TO BE A VIKING

ARRANGED BY MATT BLAIR

CROTALUS

TO BE A VIKING

Published by:
CROTALUS PUBLISHING
3500 Vicksburg Lane North #302
Plymouth, Minnesota 55447-1333
www.crotaluspublishing.com

ISBN 0-9741860-6-6

Cover and book design by Michelle L. N. Cook

Cover photo is of Matt Blair's game helmet worn during his career 1974-1986. Back cover photo is of the game ball presented to Matt Blair on September 21, 1980. Front and Back Cover photos © 2005 Martin Springborg.

Library of Congress data on record.

Crotalus and the Rattlesnake Colophon are trademarks of Crotalus Publishing.

First Printing, November 2005

Printed in Minnesota, USA

A percentage of the retail price of this book will go to benefit Special Olympics Minnesota.

Special Olympics
Minnesota

CONTENTS

ACKNOWLEDGMENTS   5

FOREWORD   6

THE OFFENSE   9
Quarterbacks
  Fran Tarkenton   10
  Tommy Kramer   13
  Brad Johnson   16
  Daunte Culpepper   19

Running Backs
  Rickey Young   23
  Ted Brown   32
  Jim Kleinsasser   36
  Michael Bennett   41
  Mewelde Moore   47

Wide Receivers
  Sammy White   52
  Nate Burleson   56
  Ryan Hoag   60

Tight Ends
  Stu Voigt   63
  Steve Jordan   65
  Jermaine Wiggins   67

Offensive Line
  Matt Birk   74
  Adam Goldberg   77
  Mick Tingelhoff   80
  Tim Irwin   86
  Randall McDaniel   90

CONTENTS

THE DEFENSE/SPECIAL TEAMS   93

Defensive Line

Jim Marshall   94

Carl Eller   103

Bob Lurtsema   112

Linebackers

Fred McNeill   120

Matt Blair   129

Scott Studwell   138

Defensive Backs

Rufus Bess   142

Joey Browner   151

Antoine Winfield   155

Darren Sharper   159

Special Teams

Darren Bennett   165

COACHES   171

Bud Grant   172

Jerry Burns   181

Mike Tice   196

PERSONNEL AND MEDIA   205

Fred Zambreletti—Head Trainer   206

Chuck Barta—Head Athletic Trainer   213

Frank Gilliam—Director of Player Personnel   215

Kirsten Lindberg—Assistant to Head Coaches   220

Bobbe Daggett—Financial   220

Dennis Ryan—Equipment Manager   227

Sid Hartman—Sports Writer,   234
Minneapolis Star Tribune

ACKNOWLEDGMENTS

A big thanks to all the players, coaches, media, and front office staff who took time to share their stories. Your kindness and support for a book on the Vikings is outstanding.

Although it's these folks who were featured, there are others who stood out in this project and also deserve my utmost thanks. Thank you to my publishing team, Dāv Kaufman and Jon Otten of Crotalus Publishing. Thanks to Michelle L. N. Cook for your work in editing and final layouts. And to my good friend Sherry Rakes, for your input and ideas.

My sincerest appreciation to the two ladies in my office at Matt Blair's Celebrity Promotions, Inc. Sara Otto, I'm thankful for all your work on a daily basis. And last, but certainly not least, to my MVP and my wife, MaryBeth, a big loving thanks for your hours and hours of work in transcribing interviews and taped conversations. You are the greatest!

You are not going to be ready to strap on the pads and suit up for a game after reading this book. It's not intended as a handbook on how to become a Viking. Its purpose is to provide you, the readers and fans, an inside look at what it means To Be a Viking.

Maybe it will serve to inspire some of you to pursue your ultimate dream of one day taking the field as a Viking. Then you'll have your own story of how you became a Viking, and it will be as different as the stories you'll find here—the stories of how Vikings greats and current players made it to the team, their time with the "Purple and Gold," and even a little on life after football. All our roads were different, but all have converged at one point in time, as we donned purple.

My road To Be a Viking began with a need for an education. As a walk-on at Northeastern A & M Junior College in Miami, Oklahoma, with God-given athletic ability, I was afforded a partial scholarship. It was my freshman summer growth spurt of three inches and forty-five pounds that paved my path to Minnesota. I transferred to Iowa State, where I overcame a senior-year knee injury before heading to the Vikings.

Captured here are stories, such as mine, that you aren't going to learn by watching the games, reading the newspaper, or even meeting a player. These are candid interviews that tell you the story behind the story.

And it was quite a process.

After producing my first book, featuring photos of some celebrity friends and benefiting the Minnesota homeless through Catholic Charities, I had dreams of publishing another photo-book. As I have worked with Special Olympics Minnesota over the last four years, I wanted to do something to benefit the inspiring athletes.

In sharing these ideas with Kathy Karkula, development director at Special Olympics Minnesota, she introduced me to Jon Otten. Jon had worked with Special Olympics through the Law Enforcement Torch Run and had connections to a publishing company.

Through Jon, I met publisher Dāv Kaufman from Crotalus Publishing. Over the course of several meetings, Dāv, Jon, and I threw around some ideas, finally deciding on a Vikings book featuring some of my original photos, plus providing a percentage of proceeds to Special Olympics Minnesota.

With the stage set, interviews started in February 2005 and continued right up until the last day prior to the big print deadline on September 1, 2005. The commitment to doing this project had no boundaries. Everywhere I went, I was making it an opportunity to talk with players.

At an autograph session in Rochester, New York, I caught up with a handful of guys. I interviewed Rickey Young in Sioux City, Iowa, during a Matt Blair's Minnesota Vikings Traveling Team Basketball game. I recorded thoughts from a few others on our way to another basketball game in Buhl, Minnesota. Various trips to Winter Park allowed me to interview many current players, including Brad Johnson about his new roll with the Vikings as backup quarterback, as well Green-Bay-Packer-turned-Viking Darren Sharper. And on a more serious note, Jim Marshall had just had back surgery, so an interview took me to his bedside. Jerry Burns was interviewed twice, as the tape recorder didn't work the first time. I caught up with my roommate of twelve years, Fred McNeill, on a recent trip to the ESPY Awards Golf Classic in California (where my team had won the 2005 ESPY Awards Golf Classic).

All their stories are different, but common themes develop. They made a commitment, respected others, had the confidence to make the right choices, preserved through tough times, stood up to peer pressure, and kept the right attitude. It takes a special person to endure, and continue to give their all as they pursue higher and higher goals.

No matter where the interviews were done, no matter the length, all should provide you with a better look at what it takes and what it means To Be a Viking.

I hope you enjoy the book as much as I enjoyed getting together with these former and current Vikings to relive the memories and dreams. And even if you aren't ready to suit up, I think I speak for everyone in this book when I say it was an honor to wear the Purple and Gold for you.

Continue to dream the ultimate dream of every Viking player, front office personnel, coaches, and every fan that the Minnesota Vikings will become World Champions. Never, never stop believing in the Purple and Gold. And I'll be right there with you, as I have been since 1974, as a Viking and season ticket holder of eight seats:

Section 117
Rows 8 and 9

Go Vikings!

Matt Blair
All-Pro #59

THE OFFENSE

#10 FRAN TARKENTON

QUARTERBACK 1961-1966, 1972-1978

Photo taken 1977

STATS

HIGH SCHOOL
Name of School: Athens High School
Location of School: Athens, Georgia
Graduation Year: 1957
Position: Quarterback
Height: 6 feet
Other sports played: Basketball and
    baseball

COLLEGE
Name of School: University of Georgia
Location of School: Atlanta, Georgia
Graduation Year: 1960
How long attended: Four years
Did you graduate? Yes
Degree: Business Administration
Position: Quarterback
Height: 6 Feet
Weight: 185 Pounds
Coach: Wallace "Wally" Butts

PRO
Position: Quarterback
Number: 10
Year Drafted: 1961
Draft Round: Third round
    (29th overall)
Year Retired: 1978
Height: 6 feet
Weight: 185 pounds
Coaches: Norm Van Brocklin and
    Bud Grant for the Vikings;
    Allie Sherman and Alex Webster
    for the Giants.

When were you drafted by the Minnesota Vikings?

I was drafted out of the University of Georgia in 1961 in the third round by the Vikings.

Where was training camp held back then?

We trained in Bemidji, Minnesota.

How many games were scheduled in Training Camp back then?

We played five exhibition games and lost them all.

What was the greatest moment for you as a young quarterback?

In 1961, we pulled off the greatest upset in National Football League history by beating the Chicago Bears 38-13. We went on to win two other games that first year, which was a tremendous accomplishment for a new franchise team of that era. The year before that, the Dallas Cowboys came into the league, played twelve games, lost eleven and tied one.

You were with the New York Giants for a time due to a trade, but you came back to the Vikings. When was that?

I was traded to the New York Giants in 1967 and spent five years there, but one of the happiest days of my life was the day I was traded back to the Vikings just before the season in 1972.

What do you think was the greatest season the Vikings had when you were with them?

The highlights of my early years were certainly the first season, but also in 1964 when we had a breakthrough year and posted our first winning record.

What are your thoughts on the Vikings playing in four Super Bowls?

We had a great run and went to four Super Bowls and, unfortunately, lost them all. I really believe if we had won one, we would have won many.

Who are some of the great players you had the opportunity to play with in that era?

I had the chance to play with some of the greatest players of that era: Jim Marshall, Alan Page, Carl Eller, Ed White, Ron Yary, Mick Tingelhoff, Grady Alderman, and Bill Brown.

What is/was your relationship with Bud Grant?

Bud Grant was a fabulous head coach. I have often made the statement if you couldn't play for Bud, you couldn't play at all.

Jerry Burns was the offensive coordinator at the time. How was your relationship with him as a coach?

Jerry Burns was our offensive coordinator, and I worked closely with him. He was the funniest human being I ever met and it was good that I had him at the end of my career, because he certainly kept things interesting. He was a great football coach.

#9   TOMMY KRAMER

QUARTERBACK   1977-1989

Photo taken 2005

STATS

HIGH SCHOOL
Name of School: Robert E. Lee High School
Location of School: San Antonio, Texas
Graduation Year: 1973
Position: Quarterback
Jersey number: 9
Height: 6 feet 2 inches
Weight: 190 pounds
40 speed: 4.8 seconds
Coach: John Ferrara
Other sports played: Baseball

COLLEGE
Name of School: Rice University
Location of School: Houston, Texas
Graduation Year: 1977
How long attended: Four years
Did you graduate? Yes
Degree: Business
Position: Quarterback
Jersey number: 9
Height: 6 feet 2 inches
Weight: 200 pounds
40 speed: 4.8 seconds
Coach: Homer Rice
Other sports played: None

PRO
Position: Quarterback
Jersey number: 9
Year Drafted: 1977
Draft Round: First
Year Retired: 1990
Height: 6 feet 2 inches
Weight: 210 pounds
40 speed: 4.9 seconds
Coach: Bud Grant, Jerry Burns, Les Steckel, Jim Morrow

What is your current job?

I'm a sales rep with United Laboratories. They're a specialty chemical manufacturer.

What was your job right after retiring from football?

I opened up a Golden Corral Steak & Family buffet-style restaurant down in San Antonio—then opened up another one. That one was in '92. Then I opened up another one five years later. I got out of the business in 2000.

What was your contract—your lowest and your highest?

My lowest base salary my rookie year was $27,500 and my highest in '89 was $1.1 million.

What was your favorite game(s) and why?

There had to be two of them. One was the San Francisco game in '77 when I came in and threw three touchdowns in the last eight minutes. We ended up winning that game 28-27 and got us into the play-offs. The next one was the Cleveland game when we went 80 yards in 14 seconds and threw the Hail-Mary pass to Ahmad [Rashad].

With that game against San Francisco, can you explain how you got the name "Two-Minute Tommy?"

Well, we had eight minutes left when Bud [Grant] put me and some of the other second-teamers in. We went right down the field in the first series and got a field goal which made it 24-7, or 24-14 at that point. Then we went right down the field again and the last two minutes of the game, I hit Sammy White with a 69-yard touchdown pass, and we ended up beating them 28-27.

How many autographs do you think you've signed over the years in your career?

Oh, I don't know . . . [laughter]. I couldn't even venture to guess. I just wish I had a dollar for each one of them though! I really don't know. I mean I've never thought about it, but I'm pretty sure it would be somewhere close to a million.

Talk about your first win against the 49ers.

Being from Texas, it was my rookie year and it's kind of cold up there, so I brought a couple sauna rocks out of the locker room with me from our sauna because we didn't have heaters on the sideline. Bud [Grant] didn't allow it, so all of a sudden, they punted the ball and, while the ball's in the air, Bud says, "Okay. You're in." So I dropped those rocks out of my pocket and damn near hit my toes trying to run out onto the field. I didn't think I was going to be able to bend my ankles. They felt like they were just locked together and, well, they eventually warmed up after that.

What do you think about the guys today compared to the guys when you played?

I think right now, well, as time goes on the players get bigger, stronger, and faster as evidenced by the size and speed of some of these guys nowadays, but I don't know, I'm sure there is a lot of the passion for the game, but it seems that coaches have to be more babysitters and motivators now than what they did back then.

Is there anything that you'd like to add to this interview?

I always liked playing outdoors. I mean there are more of the elements. I know the people hated to come up and play in Minnesota during the winter time, so I'd like to see them have a stadium up there that's outdoors—a state-of-the-art stadium and, if it's not raining, leave the roof open even if it's cold.

What is your advice to young kids and sports?

There is only one saying: "You only get out of it what you put into it." The more time and effort you put into preparing, the better you are going to get.

#14   BRAD JOHNSON

QUARTERBACK 1992-1998, 2005

Photo taken 2005

STATS

HIGH SCHOOL
Name of School: Charles D. Owen High
   School
Location of School: Black Mountain,
   North Carolina
Graduation Year: 1987
Position: Quarterback
Jersey number: 14
Height: 6 feet 3 inches
Weight: 180 pounds
40 speed: 4.9 seconds
Coach: Kenny Ford
Other sports played: Basketball

COLLEGE
Name of School: Florida State
Location of School: Tallahassee,
   Florida
Graduation Year: 1991
How long attended: Four years
Did you graduate? Yes
Degree: Physical Education
Position: Quarterback
Jersey number: 14
Height: 6 feet 5 inches
Weight: 215 pounds
40 speed: 4.9 seconds
Coach: Bobby Bowden
Other sports played: Basketball

PRO
Position: Quarterback
Jersey number: 14
Year Drafted: 1992
Draft Round: Ninth
Height: 6 feet 5 inches
Weight: 240 pounds
40 speed: 4.9 seconds
Coaches: Denny Green, Norv Turner,
   Tony Dungee, Jon Gruden, Mike
   Tice

When did you start playing football as a kid?

I started playing in third grade. It was tackle, and I played for a young league that was named the Green Bay Packers.

What position did you play?

I played right tackle. I was not a good blocker so they moved me back to running back and eventually I moved back to quarterback.

Where did you go to college? What was your best game there?

I went to Florida State. My best game was probably my first game against Virginia or probably East Carolina. I went 20-28, three touchdowns, 200 yards.

Who were you drafted by?

By the Minnesota Vikings in the ninth round. I think it was 1992.

Coming to the Vikings, who were you backing up?

When I first came here there was Wade Wilson, Rich Gannon, and Sean Salisbury so I was the third string guy that year. I was a third stringer until about 1995 and then I believe I was the backup until one of them got hurt in 1996 when I became the starter.

From there you went on to have a great career, and then you left and you moved down to Tampa. How was that experience?

I was a free agent with the Washington Redskins in 2000. Then, still as a free agent, I went to Tampa Bay. We made the playoffs in the first year but we lost. In the second year we went on and won the Super Bowl 48–21. That was an unbelievable experience. Until you've been through that experience, I don't think there's an adequate way to describe what it's like. There are only twenty-three quarterbacks that have ever won it and ten guys won it multiple times, so that was an ultimate experience and that makes you realize what a team game is about more than individual honors.

Now that you are back with the Vikings, how are you using that experience to help the Vikings?

I wish I was still in the position to be a starter, but this is a great situation with a very good football team and a really good quarterback—Daunte Culpepper who's made the Pro Bowl a couple times. It's a different experience being a backup but on the same hand, where I'm at in my career, it's also a great position and you just have to be ready to go at all times, and maybe I can bring a different concept, a different philosophy, a different thought process to the team. Daunte doesn't need any more help but maybe there are one or two ways I can help somewhere along the line. I'm just excited about another opportunity to play with a new team.

What advice do you have for kids growing up wanting to be in the NFL?

I think the biggest thing is that if you start something, you should finish it.

#11 DAUNTE CULPEPPER

QUARTERBACK 1999-PRESENT

Photo taken 2005

STATS

HIGH SCHOOL
Name of School: Vanguard High School
Location of School: Ocala, Florida
Graduation Year: 1995
Position: Quarterback
Jersey number: 8
Height: 6 feet 4 inches
Weight: 240 pounds
40 speed: 4.5 seconds
Coach: Phil Yancey
Other sports played: Basketball, baseball, and weightlifting

COLLEGE
Name of School: University of Central Florida
Location of School: Orlando, Florida
Last Year: 1998
How long attended: Four years
Did you graduate? No
Position: Quarterback
Jersey number: 11
Height: 6 feet 4 inches
Weight: 260 pounds
40 speed: 4.6 seconds
Other sports played: None

PRO
Position: Quarterback
Jersey number: 11
Year Drafted: 1999
Draft Round: 1st round
Height: 6 feet 4 inches
Weight: 264 pounds
40 speed: 4.6 seconds
Coach: Dennis Green and Mike Tice

When did you start picking up the game as a kid?

I guess the first time I started playing actual, real, organized football was when I was in the seventh grade.

What position did you play?

My first position was wide receiver.

And from wide receiver, when did you get to the quarterback side of it?

It was right after my coach actually saw me throw a ball. It was probably a couple weeks into the season.

How far did you throw it and what impressed him?

It was kind of an accident, because the quarterback at the time overthrew a pass to me, so I had to run down about another 30 yards to get the ball. I picked it up and threw it back to him about 50 yards, and I was a seventh grader. I threw it about 50-60 yards and, from that day on, I've been the quarterback.

You have a lot of records in your college days. Was there a particular game that made you realize you were going to go to the pros?

I started to get a lot of talk from scouts my freshman year. But my junior year, when we played Nebraska, they were number two in the nation, and we beat them on NBC. I think that kind of solidified me as a player in a sense and it put my name in the national audience.

How did you feel when you were picked by the Vikings as the number-one player?

I felt good. I felt blessed. I felt like I had a chance to play in the National Football League and that's what I wanted to do. I didn't care what team drafted me, and the Vikings picked me, and I was happy. The rest is history.

What goals did you set as a rookie when you came to the NFL?

I just wanted to be the best I could be. I wanted to go out and show the Vikings that they made a good decision by picking me and that was just my attitude coming into the season as a rookie.

When you came in, did you start right away or did you have anybody in front of you?

Well, I came in during a unique situation. Randall Cunningham was here. Jeff George was here. I came in as a third quarterback, and a lot of people speculated that I wouldn't play until three to four years down the road. Coach Green granted me my wish, and I became the starting quarterback my second year.

You've grown over the years and your game has improved. What made the difference of you becoming a better quarterback now?

Just me getting more experience and being more calm in the pocket and just learning the ins and outs of the position. Studying film and just working hard basically. A lot of hard work.

Can you share a little about your upbringing in Florida?

Well, I was adopted when I was one day old by a very beautiful woman named Emma Culpepper. My mom was in prison at the time, and she called her and asked Emma to take me until she got out. When my mom got out about four years later, I didn't know her at all, you know. I wanted to stay with my real mom—I mean my mom who adopted me. But I did go with my biological mom for about a week or so and she saw how unhappy I was, so she took me back to my adopted mom. She moved up to Ocala from Miami so she could be close to me, even though I didn't live with her, she wanted to be close to me and wanted to be in my life.

And you've volunteered at an adoption agency here?

When I came up to Minnesota, I wanted to get into some type of charity. I didn't know what I wanted at first and then as I looked around, the African American Adoption Agency became clear to me that that's where I wanted to work. Being African American myself, I felt like it would be a great fit. Everything's been very smooth and very good.

Do you have a family here, and how many kids do you have?

Yes, I'm married to my high school sweetheart, Kimberly Culpepper, and we have five beautiful kids.

Are you getting them into sports at this time?

My three oldest are girls, and they haven't gotten into it. They're really girly, but my two youngest are boys, and my oldest boy is three years old, and he's loving any type of ball right now. He's throwing it, hitting it, running it, and my youngest is nine months old, and he's got a little ways to go yet but . . .

What advice do you have for young kids in sports and education?

Just be the best you can be in everything you can. It doesn't matter what situation you're in at the current moment. It's all about being the best and striving to be the best. It's not where you're at, it's where you're going.

#34 RICKEY YOUNG

RUNNING BACK 1978-1983

Photo taken 1978

STATS

HIGH SCHOOL
Name of School: C.F. Vigor High School
Location of School: Mobile, Alabama
Graduation Year: 1971
Position: Running Back
Jersey number: 29
Height: 5 feet 11 inches
Weight: 180 pounds
40 speed: 4.6 seconds
Coach: Harold Clark
Other sports played: Baseball

COLLEGE
Name of School: Jackson State
Location of School: Jackson, Mississippi
Graduation Year: 1975
How long attended: Four years
Did you graduate? Yes
Degree: Business
Position: Running Back
Jersey number: 35
Height: 6 feet 2 inches
Weight: 203 pounds
40 speed: 4.5 seconds
Coach: Robert Hill
Other sports played: None

PRO
Position: Running Back
Jersey number: 34
Year Drafted: 1975
Draft Round: Seventh
Year Retired: 1984
Height: 6 feet 2 inches
Weight: 208 pounds
40 speed: 4.6 seconds
Coach: Bud Grant

When did you start getting into football?
I started playing football when I was in sixth or seventh grade.

What position did you play?
Back then I played linebacker and defensive back.

When you were a kid, were you big, small, or in-between?
I would say probably in-between. Tall and maybe a little on the thin side.

What sports did you play in high school?
I played baseball, ran a little track, and football.

What did you run in track?
I ran in the 4x4 relay and, back then, they called it the 220. Now I think they call it the 200 meter.

What college did you go to and did you get there on a scholarship?
Yes. I think I was up to be drafted to be in Vietnam, but my grandmother didn't want me to go into the Army, so she personally drove me up to Jackson State College. One of my old friends got a scholarship there and talked the coach into giving me a tryout. I tried out, made it, and had four great years in college at Jackson State.

When was the point for you in college when you knew you were going to be a professional player?
You work hard and you knew that somebody had to be watching. I played a lot and was really a blocking back for my roommate and nephew through marriage (Walter Payton), but most of the time, we were ahead so far, the coach would put me in at running back

---

and a guy named Rodney Phillips, from the Rams, would be my blocking back—so I got to play a bit. But you know, you have to prepare for it. It's like I tell my kids, if you prepare and you work hard, you have to be lucky and you got to cash in when you get your opportunity, so I was fortunate enough to get drafted in the seventh round at San Diego, and that gave me a shot, and it's worked out really well for me.

When were you traded to the Vikings?

In 1978 for Ed White.

How was your first year in training camp in San Diego?

It was a learning experience. You know what's funny is that we had a coach in college who used to practice us in Jackson, Mississippi—the weather was always hot. We'd go out at night and practice three times a day. I remember the first day of practice in San Diego, when the coach blew the whistle and everybody came in, I thought we really are going to start practicing now. And the coach said, "Let's take it in. It's a little hot out here today." I just laughed at them.

So training camp in San Diego was a cake walk compared to college?

Yeah! Absolutely. The plays and terminology were new so it was kind of a stressful situation. You want to make the team, but you know you're not a high draft choice, and there's just so much stuff you have to learn in such a short period of time. You only have so much time to show them that you can play. You've got to be really prepared for that next level. They worked us hard, but we were ready and in shape.

What was the hardest thing for you to grasp once you came to the NFL?

The thing is, you learn one terminology in high school, then you go to the next level and everyone does it a little faster. How well you do it and how well you prepare yourself mentally is what separates you from the others. They know your talent, so the rest is just a matter of applying yourself and working hard so when the opportunity comes, you get in there, you're prepared, and you can do what you're supposed to do.

Who were some of the players that made the team that year as a rookie?

Let's see, we had a great year that year. Gary Johnson from Grambling, Louis Kelcher from Southern Methodist, Fred Dean from Louisiana Tech, and Mike Williams from LSU. He wasn't a good coach, but he knew talent. Billy Shields from Georgia Tech. Everybody's from the south it seems—like the southern connection or something. Hall-of-famer Dan Foust was there. We had Charlie Joyner from Grambling but he was there three to four years ahead of us. We had a good team. We could go out and score 40 points and then lose 40-41! Okay, maybe the last year we could score points, but we didn't stop anybody. Give the defense some props. We had a practice defense, but we had some players who could play. We just had some discipline problems. But other than that, we had people who could play, and we had fun out there.

How did you come to be a Viking?

At that time, San Diego was going through a lot of ownership problems and they told me I had to sign at least a three-year contract. Walter Payton and I had the same attorney, and he told me that if I play for them, they'd tear up my contact and redo it. But then they made some promises they weren't willing to keep—it was a mess. I remember the first game I played in Minnesota: I had just come from San Diego and didn't even have an overcoat. It was funny. I remember freezing and talking to Sid, who was San Diego's equipment manager, telling him I ain't ever been that cold in my life. I think after that, San Diego punished me by trading me back here. But it was the best thing that ever happened to me. I'm sure I got a couple more years out of my career. Bud [Grant] was a kind of a no-nonsense guy. You knew if he liked you or not. You just played. I respected him for that.

How was the Vikings' training camp different from San Diego's?

Well, like I said, Bud [Grant]'s no nonsense. He didn't run you a whole lot and he didn't work you too hard because you had to come in prepared yourself. If you weren't ready to go, he'd just replace you and keep the ball moving. If the crew is not ready to sail, the ship will sail without you. Here, the terminology and everything was a lot more relaxed, and I'm glad I made it.

You and Fran Tarkenton received the record for most completed passes. What year was that, and how many passes did you catch that season?

It was 1978. I was fortunate enough to play with two Hall of Fame quarterbacks, [Dan] Fouts and Fran. The difference between Fouts was that, although they were both great players, Fouts could throw a ball through a needle, and Fran would just get the ball to you in so many different ways, and he just knew what would happen before it happened on the field. I caught 88 passes that year—that's a lot of passes, let me tell you. Chuck Foreman had 61. I think the record still holds. Between the two of us, we had a combined record of 149 receptions.

What was the coldest game you played?

There's no question. It was here against Kansas City—the last game at Met Stadium. It was so cold. It was trying to rain and started to snow and it changed three different ways. I think it snowed, and then turned to sleet, and then back to rain. I was never so cold in my life. And through it all, they beat us 17–31 or something like that. That was back in 1981. It was the last game because we were in the dome in 1982.

How many years did you play in the Dome?

Two years. 1982-83.

What goals did you set in your career and did you accomplish them?

You always try to set goals. I felt fortunate to be out there, and I always knew that I met people along the way who could help me, and I knew that was important, so I was able to do some things for my parents and my grandmother, and I was really proud of that and really thankful for the opportunities I had. A lot of people have to help you along the way to get you to this point. You have to be fortunate, and you have to be prepared, but the goals that I set were trying to give back to the community, and I think I accomplished that.

What was your fondest memory of Met Stadium?

There are a lot of them out there. I remember the first year I was here, we were playing the Bears and it was so cold. I was trying to slide over where the benches were to get warmed up and unknowingly got too close to a heater flame and it set my cape on fire. At that point there was a turnover and Bud [Grant] was looking around for me and I was dancing on the sidelines with the back of my cape on fire! The people in the stands were laughing and eventually I got it out. But that was one of the fondest memories out there—catching on fire as I was ready to go out on the field after trying to get warmed up!

What was the funniest thing that happened to you in training camp?

In training camp, let's see, we were always messing with Burnsie [Jerry Burns]. Burnsie is pretty funny. I was always asleep in the meeting rooms so they always made me sit by him and run the projector. A couple of times he was running it and one time he broke it and he got pissed off at me and told Bud I broke the film on purpose so I'd get out of meetings! Bud made me stay after practice and run just because of Burnsie.

What do you think it takes to be a Viking these days?

So many things have changed with the free agency, which is a good thing. I can't blame the players, but the one thing that it doesn't allow them to do is to play long enough together to get some continuity, you know, to know what the next guy is going to do and when. Everybody knew everybody else's abilities because you played long enough together in a more family atmosphere. Now a guy changes from team to team to team so much that you miss some of the continuity and you miss some of the camaraderie. When we played, you came to a team, you got drafted and stayed there unless they wanted to trade you. Otherwise you were kind of stuck there, so it's good and it's bad. I think it's bad for the fans in the sense that it's kind of a revolving door for them. You know you're booing a guy one week and the next week you got to cheer for him, so that part of it I don't like. But I do respect the guys who are getting paid, because your career could end in warm-ups, so there are a lot of things that can happen to you as a player, and I feel good that these guys are getting paid the way they should be paid. I just don't know if they really appreciate it as much as I think they should. But otherwise, you've got to be a really strong and motivated individual to stay at that high a level these days. They pay you a ton of dough and there are a lot of things you can do to prepare yourself to come out and play every Sunday. So that part of it is tough.

What advice would you give to kids on sports and education?

Go to school and get an education over everything else and focus on the things that are important. Get involved in a team sport because it teaches you so many things in life. Stay focused and follow your dreams and, if you aspire to do something, stick with it. A lot of good things happen for people with hard work.

What is your take on the Randy Moss deal for leaving the team and being traded?

The one thing that I was so disappointed in Randy is when he walked off the field with time still left on the clock. As a team, you live and you die together. You have to learn how to win and how to sometimes lose. To get where you want to be, you got to do some things you don't want to do. There are some adverse things that happen but you're not the only person around. If you're playing on a team sport, you've got to depend on everybody to do their job and sometimes you get frustrated, but more than not, if you're a real team player, and you get lucky and get on a good team, it's one of the best experiences you could ever have. I think someone forgot that.

Who on the team did you hang out with?

I hung out a lot with [Tommy] Kramer with the Vikings, and got in trouble every once in awhile. There's a lot of people. I hate to say one or two, but Ahmad [Rashad], Chuck [Foreman]. I had a few people I hung out with.

What do you miss the most now that you're retired?

I'm sure with everybody, you miss going to the locker room and just the camaraderie. Even the drudgery of going to training camp and practice, you look back and say, "Did I do the best I could? Did I get the most out of it?" And you think, yeah, in some way I guess I did, so that's the thing I miss the most about it. When you win everyone is happy and when you lose, you know, everyone is still in the same boat. You learn to live with each other in a whole different sense than family. But you spend so much time together; they just become a part of your family.

What was your lowest and your highest contract?

The lowest was in San Diego—it was either play or walk to the gas station and make more money, so I stuck it out. I would say probably when I started in San Diego, it was about $38,000 and when I left it was about $175,000 with everything.

What do you do right now as a current job?

I'm partners with two other gentlemen in a mortgage company. We've been in business for five years. We're downtown Minneapolis off of Washington, and its going really good for us.

When you retired, was the transition from a Viking to a businessman a struggle?

Absolutely. It takes a little time to get back into the real world because you're used to having everybody do everything for you all the time, agents, etc. When you retire from professional football, you really have to go out and butt heads for real in the competition out there in the job markets. It's a whole different world. And yes, you do struggle. You try to find your way just like everyone else.

#23   TED BROWN

RUNNING BACK   1979-1986

Photo taken 2005

STATS

HIGH SCHOOL
Name of School: High Point Andres High School

Location of School: High Point, North Ca[rolina]

Graduation Year: 1975

Position: Halfback

Jersey number: 40

Height: 5 feet 9 inches

Weight: 175 pounds

40 speed: 4.5 seconds

Coach: Bob Boswell—he also was my co[llege] assistant coach

Other sports played: Basketball, track

COLLEGE
Name of School: North Carolina State University

Location of School: Raleigh, North Carolina

Graduation Year: 1978

How long attended: Four years

Did you graduate? Yes, from Metro State University

Degree: Human Services, minor in Counseling

Position: Halfback, Tailback

Jersey number: 23

Height: 5 feet 10 inches

Weight: 193 pounds

40 speed: 4.3 seconds

Coach: Lou Holtz (first year), Bo Rein (three years)

Other sports played: Track and Field

PRO
Position: Running Back

Jersey number: 23

Year Drafted: 1979

Draft Round: First

Year Retired: 1986

Height: 5 feet 10 inches

Weight: 210 pounds

40 speed: I never ran the 40-yard dash. Never went to The Combine.

Coach: Bud Grant, Les Steckel, and Jerry Burns. I had Bud coach twice.

What is your current job?
Right now I'm a probation officer for Ramsey County—a juvenile probation officer—have been doing that for the last ten years.

What is your favorite Vikings game and why?
My favorite Vikings game is the game we played against the Cleveland Browns. I think it was 1980. We were down by three touchdowns, and we came back and had a Hail Mary at the end where Ahmad Rashad caught the ball and backed into the end zone. We won the division and went on to the playoffs.

Lead us to the point to where the Hail Mary was thrown.
You know, we had 80 yards to go and basically we did what we call a "flea flicker" but we'd be working on this play—none of the wide receivers knew what we were gonna do—so we didn't tell them. They were running hard down the field and gave us that space and in the "flea flicker" we threw the ball to Joe Senser and he flipped it back to me, and I had the presence of mind to run out of bounds at about the 50-yard line and gave us a chance for that last play.

What is your lowest and highest contract in your career?
Mike Lynn, the former general manager, told us "look we got a season ticket here that's for thirty years. You'll take what we give you." But I think the lowest one was about $30,000 and the highest was about $400,000.

How many autographs do you think you've signed over your career?
Somewhere close to probably about 750,000. I got in the game a little bit late as far as signing autographs and stuff like that, but over the last ten years I've signed quite a few, so I'm gonna say about 750,000.

What do you think about grass and turf?

I like grass better. I played my whole high school and college career on grass, and I hate turf because that's how I got hurt. I tore my knee up on turf, so definitely grass. Grass is a better thing. They should outlaw turf.

What do you think about women in the locker rooms as reporters?

I think that it's not a good idea, but I don't think they should limit women from having access to the players, but there should be a time and place where they can get their interviews and stuff when the players are fully dressed. I don't agree with women being in the locker room when guys have towels on and are half undressed, you know? But I don't think they should limit them either, though. So I think they should give them full access, but once the players are dressed.

If you were to add anything to your career, what would you share with your fans?

I would like to share that if I could add one thing I would have added that I should have made the Pro Bowl because you can't beat catching 83 passes and not make it to the Pro Bowl. That's kind of unheard of, but you know sometimes the Pro Bowl is politics. But if I could add one thing that's what I have to add. And also a championship.

Playing in your time and playing today, what do you think about it and how do you compare the two?

While I think when I played in the late '70s and early '80s, I think that it was more about the game than about how much paper you got or how many diamonds you got or how many Cadillac Escalades you can drive. I think the players right now are pretty spoiled and they get some ridiculous things. I'm not mad at them for what they get; I'm saying more power to them. But I think the game has changed quite a bit over the past twenty years. I think the players that played back in the '60s and '70s felt more about the game, and they wanted to play the game better than the kids do now. The young kids nowadays get all this money and they get all this prestige, and I think they spend more time seeing how many cars they can drive versus going out studying the game and being a part of the game and knowing different positions. I doubt you can go to one player or two players now and say "what does the tackle do on this play," if he's a wide receiver. I betcha that wide receivers don't know what the tackle does or how they protect him so he can get the ball. So, back then I think we studied the game a lot better.

If you were giving advice to young kids, what would you tell them as they are growing up today and thinking about sports?
First of all, they need to understand that sport is a short-lived game and basically they should get their education first—think about graduating from college first before even talking about playing ball. Because it's almost like the more you make, the more you spend. They can take away football, but they can't take away your education. And I think they first should deal with their education and then deal with the football. But I don't know though with the money they make these days, you can buy you some education I guess. I don't know. I just think be set in your education first and then go into what sport it is you're trying to play.

#40 JIM KLEINSASSER

RUNNING BACK 1999-PRESENT

Photo taken 2005

STATS

HIGH SCHOOL
High School: Carrington High
Location of School: Carrington, North
 Dakota
Graduation Year: 1995
Position: Tight End, Running Back,
 Linebacker, Defensive End
Jersey number: 81
Height: 6 feet 3 inches
Weight: 240 pounds
Coach: Marty Huchhalter
Other sports played: Basketball, track

COLLEGE
Name of School: University of North Dakota
Location of School: Grand Forks, North
 Dakota
Last Year of College: 1998
How long attended: 4 years
Did you graduate? No
Major: Finance
Position: Tight End
Jersey number: 82
Height: 6 feet 3 inches
Weight: 270 pounds
40 speed: 4.56 seconds
Coach: Roger Thomas
Other sports played: Basketball

PRO
Position: Tight end
Jersey number: 40
Year Drafted: 1999
Draft Round: Second
Height: 6 feet 3 inches
Weight: 273 pounds
40 speed: 4.56 seconds
Coach: Dennis Green and Mike Tice

What title is your position? What does "stageback" mean and can you explain what that position really is?

It's kind of a cross between the old fullback and a tight end where you not just sit on the line, but you move around quite a bit in the formations and in the motions. You do a lot more things in the pass protection game and with the run blocking for the backfield, up on the line. You are all over the place—on the line, off the line. It's more of a motion-type position.

It's kind of like the fullback position?

Yeah. You don't see a lot of fullbacks anymore and it's kind of a way to keep your personnel tight and mix it up. You can see what kind of package you've got coming with the tight end to the line or you can put him back and two backs set so, it kind of works well that way.

When did you get the indication that you'd like to be a professional football player?

I always dreamed of it while playing in the backyard pretending I was on the Washington Redskins with my uniform on. It never really crept into my mind, you know? I never really thought I had a shot until my junior year in college when I got some feedback from some scouts. It's always been something that I wanted to do, so it never really hit my mind as reality until then.

Did you play any other sports besides football?

In high school I played basketball and track, and my freshman year in college I played basketball too. But after a year, I decided that football was where my future rested.

During the course of your career, when did you feel like you established yourself as a consistent player? Do you remember that game or that play?

The first three years I was playing a fullback position, and it wasn't until Mike Tice switched me back to the tight end, halfback set and probably that first game back against Chicago, playing that halfback, tight end position exclusively is when I felt like I was where I belonged. That was my fourth year and is what got me there.

What do you like to do more—catch or run the ball?

Probably catch because of the way my body is running. It's pretty much just run straightforward up the field. I don't have any illusions I have any cutting ability, so I don't want to take a pounding into the line and get my knees taken out.

What part of the week is your favorite besides game times?

Well besides that, probably Friday. You're still getting hyped up for the games, it's a half day, and you review all the hard work you've done Wednesday and Thursday. You have the chance to relax a little bit and kind of let go for a little bit and just hang out with the guys.

Who's your roommate on the road when you travel?

Sean Berton was my roommate last year in training camp, but I didn't travel at all last year. In the past it was always Chris Walsh, and two years ago it was Hunter Goodwin.

What's your favorite meal or food?

I like a good steak. My family raised beef and we used to grill hamburgers and steaks pretty much every night, so I'm pretty much a steak fiend.

Pre-game meal, what do you like to eat?

A couple chicken breasts and a small serving of pasta. I like to keep it light. Maybe a little cookie at the end and then just a ton of water.

Before coming to the pros, what did you go through to get to where you're at physically?

Well, going through college sets you in the mood for what you have to do, but after all is done, I went down to Dallas and worked out with Bob King and got ready for the draft that way. Just coming in here and absorbing what everyone else was doing, you take a little bit from each person you meet along the way and you kind of blend them all together.

Who is Bob King and what does he do for the pros?

He's a trainer down in Dallas. I met him down in Dallas with my agent. In North Dakota, it's kind of tough to go out and get on a field and throw some balls in January—we didn't have any indoor facilities, so we went down there.

Which was you favorite Vikings game?

There are quite a few. Maybe when we just beat the Packers—that was a great game. I'm still waiting for my greatest to be at the Super Bowl. I'm holding out on that.

Do you set any goals?

Oh yeah, definitely. It's just like anything else; you set goals for limiting your mistakes, being sharp, etc. The biggest thing is just taking care of your business down the line, doing your job no matter what it is—blocking, catching. I keep mine pretty straight and narrow. I don't set goals to catch so many balls. I mean, I keep it general, you know, as long as it's something to get us to the championship.

Do you have a favorite charity that you work with?

I work with Special Olympics in Jamestown. It's kind of my regional area back home. We do a banquet every year and some fundraising stuff. And up here, I'm usually the honorary chairman and a board member for the Make-A-Wish Foundation.

Any thoughts that you want to give to kids getting ready to participate in sports?

The biggest thing is hard work. Hard work will make up for a lot of things you don't currently have. That goes not just for sports—that goes for anything. If you want to be something, just go out and do it.

How was your knee injury? Are you going to be ready to be on schedule for this year?

Definitely. Right now I'm going through full workouts with the team. I'm feeling great and, come training camp, I shouldn't have any memories of this injury at all.

#23 MICHAEL BENNETT

RUNNING BACK   2001-PRESENT

Photo taken 2005

STATS

HIGH SCHOOL
Name of School: Milwaukee Tech
Location of School: Milwaukee, Wisconsin
Graduation Year: 1998
Position: Running Back
Jersey number: 41
Height: 5 feet 9 inches
Weight: 195 pounds
40 speed: 4.25 seconds
Coach: Tom Konowalski, Billy Harris
Other sports played: Track and field

COLLEGE
Name of School: University of Wisconsin
Location of School: Madison, Wisconsin
Graduation Year: 2001
How long attended: 3 1/2 years
Did you graduate? No
Position: Running Back
Jersey number: 29
Height: 5 feet 10 inches
Weight: 204 pounds
40 speed: 4.19 seconds
Coach: Barry Alverez
Other sports played: Track and field

PRO
Position: Running Back
Jersey number: 23
Year Drafted: 2001
Draft Round: First
Height: 5 feet 10 inches
Weight: 208 pounds
40 speed: 4.25 seconds
Coach: Dennis Green, Mike Tice

How many people are in your family?
Just my mom, my sister, and me. So it's just the three of us.

At what age did you become interested in football?
I think I was about four or five when I really started to notice it. I watched my uncles playing high school football, college and professional football, so they were kind of like my father figures growing up. I wanted to be just like them or better and fortunately I was able to get to this position I am now because of them.

What are their names and what teams did they play for?
My oldest uncle was Charles Bennett and he played defensive end with the Bears, then the Cowboys and he retired with the Dolphins. My other uncle was Tony Bennett and was a first round pick for the Green Bay Packers in '90. He played linebacker and defensive end, then went on to play with the Indianapolis Colts and went on to retire in '93.

You broke a lot of records in high school. What was your proudest game?
I think it was my freshman year when I started on varsity, and in my first game I had 300 yards rushing in maybe ten carries. Every time I got the ball it was like a long run. That was the biggest thing that probably set me in the frame of mind that if I just did right in school, there was no saying how far I could go with football.

Were there any other schools you wanted to go to besides Wisconsin?
I looked at Michigan, Florida, Florida State but most of my family was there in Wisconsin after we had made the journey up from Mississippi. I just wanted to be around the kids I went to high

school with and grew up around and I didn't want to travel too far. Madison is only forty-five minutes, give or take, from Milwaukee.

What was the game that really made you know you had made it?

I think it was a lot of games. It was kind of great for me to go in and sit behind a great running back in Ron Dayne and watch him. Also another running back who was there was Eddie Falkner. I got a chance to learn from those guys and grow. I got involved with my strength coaches, Ron Detman, my running back coach Brian White. And as I got more familiar with the college game I was able to come in and play. I backed up Ron Dayne, so I played sparingly, but I did special teams and stuff like that. I then came to a point where it was my time to shine and I think my biggest game was against Oregon. I think I had 23 carries for 308 yards that game, so right then I knew it was my time to do what I had to do to get to this point in my life.

Did you run track in high school and carry it on to college?

Well I ran AAU track and started when I was six so I've been running for twenty years—I'm twenty-six now. I've been running for a long time. I felt it was something like a hobby, I felt I could always win every race, so I did it for fun. As I grew older, things didn't really start getting serious for me until I was in high school. I won a lot of national trophies at a young age but once I got to high school the competition was stiffer. I was able to go out and win and still set a lot of records. It came down to that it was either football or track, but my heart is in football. In track, I like to win and I like winning gold medals, so that was one of the things that kind of kept me going and it helped with football. It helped me to get my speed down. When I went on to college, I had the chance to go to the Olympics my junior year, but I stayed to play football because that's really where my heart was and I was running track just as a hobby.

What did you run and what was your fastest time?

I ran the 100, 200 and 4x100 relay. My fastest time in the 100 was a 9.93, my fastest 200 time was a 20.18.

How did you feel when you were drafted by the Vikings?

I felt good. I really felt good being a first-round pick. It was just one of those things I was hoping for, and it happened for me. Like I said, right now I'm living a childhood dream come true. I'm living in it day to day. I know that a lot of people aren't fortunate enough to be in the situation I was able to be in. It's just a great feeling for me but I'm still living a day at a time.

How did the veterans treat you coming to training camp as a rookie?

I think the biggest veteran for me was getting to know Talance Sawyer. As soon as I got in, he took me under his wing and was showing me around, showing me different places to go, and just covering the ropes of the NFL. My rookie year at training camp was not as good as the last two years because Corey Stringer passed in my rookie year and it really took the breath out of training camp, you know. It was a rough one for me early on but time went on, things started to calm down—it was still something that was always in the back of your mind. You get to thinking that if I'm working this hard, will it happen to me? We're all put on this earth for a purpose and I'm still living my life now and I'm very happy, but early in my career . . . it's something that will always be with me.

Were there any jokes played on you in training camp?

There definitely were, there were a lot of jokes. I think I got the biggest one during the season, though. I didn't know you weren't supposed to wear your good clothes over here, so once it got cold, they dipped all my jeans and t-shirts and everything in water and hung it out on the goal posts and we had a snowstorm. They also rolled all my windows down and parked my car up on top of the hill and turned the AC on. That's probably the most abuse that I've got.

What about Thanksgiving Day? Did they make you get some turkeys?

You know what? Thanksgiving Day wasn't too bad for me. I got to spend it with my family, which was good. So actually as far as I can remember, it was pretty good. My thing was having to go get chicken and bring it on the plane, and pay for all the guys when we go out to eat. That was my biggest thing but I've got rookies to do that for me now, so I'm pretty happy.

During the week, besides game day, is there a day of the week that you look forward to?

If it's during the summer time, right up to early September, I look forward to coming in here early enough so I can get out of here and get on my boat and go fishing. I love to fish. It relaxes me and gets me away from everything. I can just be out on the water and really not have to concentrate. Just sit out on the water and throw my line in and, hopefully, whatever I catch, I catch.

What's your biggest fish you've caught?

A twelve-pound largemouth bass—at Lake Okeechobee down in Florida.

Have you done any deep sea fishing?

Definitely. My uncle, Tony Bennett, is from Oakland, and he's an average fisherman. Now that he's retired, he's a big outdoorsman so when I go down to Florida, I get with him and we go out and get mahi-mahi, marlin, shark. Whatever is out there in the water, we're trying to catch it.

Do you have a foundation or some type of charity that you represent?

I'm big in the Boys and Girls Club. Also my AAU track club which is in Milwaukee, Wisconsin. It's part of Milwaukee's pride and it's run by Coach Sims, my track coach. Between those two, I really am into the D.A.R.E. flag football here locally in Minneapolis.

What's your favorite food?

I'm a snack food guy. My favorite food of all time? I'd say pizza. I could do pepperoni and sausage combination pizza any day of the week.

What advice would you have for kids about school, football, or anything else?

Well, just for the fans, or for the parents first. As your kids are growing up, try and encourage them, try to be there for everything that they are involved in, no matter if it's the violin, basket weaving or anything because as a young man growing up without a father really hurt me in a way because I would always have to bring my mom to my games—you know, my mom had to be mother and father. So to single parents out there, support your kids no matter what. To the younger generation: listen to your parents. Get around somebody who has been down the hard roads, who can give you great advice, and surround yourself with good people and good things will happen.

#30   MEWELDE MOORE

RUNNING BACK 2004-PRESENT

Photo taken 2005

STATS

HIGH SCHOOL
Name of School: Belaire High School
Location of School: Baton Rouge, Louisiana
Graduation Year: 2000
Position: Running Back, Wide Receiver, Defensive Back, Linebacker
Jersey number: 21
Height: 5 feet 8 inches
Weight: 190 pounds
40 speed: 4.4 seconds
Coach: Barry Amadee
Other sports played: Baseball, basketball

COLLEGE
Name of School: Tulane University
Location of School: New Orleans, Louisiana
Graduation Year: 2004
How long attended: 4 years
Did you graduate? Yes
Degree: Finance, Accounting
Position: Running Back
Jersey number: 26
Height: 5 feet 10 inches
Weight: 208 pounds
40 speed: 4.4 seconds
Coach: Chris Seelfo
Other sports played: Baseball (San Diego)

PRO
Position: Running Back
Jersey number: 30
Year Drafted: 2004
Draft Round: Fourth
Height: 5 feet 11 inches
Weight: 212 pounds
40 speed: 4.4 seconds
Coach: Mike Tice

When did you start thinking about playing professional football?

I think I had those little hutch pads, those little Halloween costumes with the New Orleans Saints and LSU. That was back in '87. So I guess I was about five or six years old.

How many siblings do you have?

I have two brothers, two sisters, and a step-sister. So that's three sisters and two brothers—six of us, all together.

Were you the only one to come to the pros?

Yeah, I'm the only one so far.

So you have younger brothers?

Yeah, I have a younger brother who is three and a younger sister who is five.

In college, what would you say was your breakout game that put you into the pros?

I think it's all the big games I played. I mean, you can take anyone . . . playing BYU, playing Texas, playing LSU, Mississippi State. It's all those games that just proves that being a mid-major team playing a major team, and putting numbers up like that, I knew I could play in the next level.

Did you have a mentor/coach who encouraged you to put forth the effort to become a pro?

Not really. They just knew I wanted to do it. They could see it in me. They could see it in my work ethic and, you know, my whole thing was I never really had to put pressure on the coaches. They always knew that I just did what I had to do. I made their job easy. I just stayed out of trouble, stayed on top of my school work, and it was no problem. It was like, here's this guy's stuff, here's his resume and everything you see. Believe it.

How did it feel to be in training camp as a rookie and what was your bright spot in training camp?

In training camp, you know, it's just an every day thing and you just got to go out there and make a play. And I think every day I just went out there and made a play.

Did any of the veterans help you along the way on your plays?

They asked me to do just anything. You know, whatever they asked me to do, I just decided if I was going to do it. I never really complained about what was going on, I just knew I wanted to go out there and play. I wanted to be coachable.

Did you have any goals coming into the pros?

I had a lot of goals. I mean, you always want to start, you want to be "the guy," you want to do a lot of things. But the number one thing, my goal was to be humble enough to understand that I'm at the bottom of the totem pole, you know, honestly earn my keep and pay my dues.

What was your best game that you felt contributed to the Vikings' winning streak last year in the 2004 season?

I think I did a lot. I mean, they basically gave me the opportunity coming in almost at the halfway point during the season. We were like three running backs down who couldn't play. One wasn't ready and there were just two of us and basically they just came up to me and said, "Here's your shot, let's see what you got." It came down to me getting the opportunity to play. They knew they could rely on me. They could count on me.

Which games did you start?

I started Houston Texans, New Orleans Saints, Tennessee Titans, and New York Giants.

Now that you've had a year under your belt, are you looking to be the number one starter?
No. Now that my feet are wet and everything, I just want to go in and look to make plays and do whatever I need to do to get on that field.

What do you think about Minnesota so far?
Minnesota is just a beautiful place. You know, everything about it—the fans, the atmosphere, you know, just living, being around here. It kind of reminds me of Baton Rouge and New Orleans. It's the same kind of comparison to where I live in the downtown area, but this is a much cleaner environment, and I enjoy it. I'm having fun, and just taking my time, making sure I stay out of trouble and every day I try to learn something new. Whether it's reading a book on finance where gurus talk about how you make money or looking at plays or out there playing the game, I'm just always trying to find ways, mentally and physically, to better myself.

Is there any future you're thinking about right now, or are you just concentrating on football? Or are you thinking about a particular business or job you want to have once you retire?
Well, right now, my interests are in real estate and restaurants. But I want to know what I'm doing, what I'm getting into a little bit more. So right now, I'm just learning and I'm just trying to understand the industry, and once I get a better grasp on how things work in the industry, I'll be able to get in there and make a good transition.

What would you like to see happening with the Vikings in their play this year?
I would like to win the Super Bowl. I mean, that's it. There ain't nothing else outside of that. If you win the Super Bowl, then everything else comes after that. The bottom line is Super Bowl.

What's your favorite food?

Well, it's my mom's rice and gravy, but she doesn't like to make it. And baked chicken and some corn bread. I'm making myself hungry right now . . .

Do you have a favorite charity?

Actually, one thing is Brights and Tide and that's my main goal. I want to make sure that I stay in the background—my religious background—that's 10 percent of my earnings. And I'm getting into that aspect of my life. I also want to make sure I give back to kids right now so I go to schools and talk to people who are less fortunate, just to give them a better outlook to help them understand that, in this world, there's nothing that comes easy, no matter what you do. You have to work for it.

You're a huge baseball fan, right?

Definitely, I'm a huge baseball fan. I love baseball. I love football more than I love baseball, that's why I'm playing football. It's a great game. It's a great sport, and I enjoy it.

What's your favorite team?

The Boston Red Sox.

Any advice you have for kids going into sports?

I'll just say education is the most important thing. Nobody can take away your mind. When you put God first, and say your prayers at night, and every day you work to get better, you work to do things that are positive. Keep a positive attitude, always have a good attitude and have a good approach about things, and no matter what type of negativity you are approached by, you are still your own person, you still make your own decisions. Be optimistic and positive about your decisions. Try to think about things you do before you actually do them.

#85   SAMMY WHITE

WIDE RECEIVER   1976-1986

Photo taken 2005

STATS

HIGH SCHOOL
Name of School: Richwood High School
Location of School: Monroe, Louisiana
Graduation Year: 1972
Position: Running Back, Receiver
Jersey number: 25
Height: 5 feet 10 inches
Weight: 185 pounds
40 speed: 4.6 seconds
Coach: Eugene Hughs
Other sports played: Baseball

COLLEGE
Name of School: Grambling State University
Location of School: Grambling, Louisiana
Graduation Year: 1976
How long attended: Four years
Did you graduate? Yes
Degree: Physical Education
Position: Wing Back and Receiver
Jersey number: 26
Height: 5 feet 11 inches
Weight: 194 pounds
40 speed: 4.6 seconds
Coach: Eddie Robinson
Other sports played: None

PRO
Position: Wide Receiver
Jersey number: 85
Year Drafted: 1976
Draft Round: Second
Year Retired: 1986
Height: 5 feet 11 inches
Weight: 200 pounds
40 speed: 4.6 seconds
Coach: Bud Grant

What did you do when you retired from the Vikings? What was your first job?

My first job after I retired from the Vikings was working for a company called Georgia Pacific. I managed a boxing plant where you get boxes all over the country for tires and vegetables. You name it, we made a box for it.

What is your current job now?

Currently, I am coaching at my alma mater, Grambling State University. Presently, I'm their receiving coach and offensive coordinator, and I've been there about eight years.

What are your good and bad memories from training camp?

There's a lot of those! But the good memory is that they always had the best food. You could eat good three meals a day. The first bad memory is that it's really tough to pinpoint. I think it was the year we had Les Steckel as head coach. He drove us as though we were Marines.

What would you rather play on, turf or grass?

Grass. Astroturf, when you tackle or catch a ball—or not catch a ball—you're going to get beat up. Grass, you know, gives and Astroturf just seems to just stay in one place. Many people have lost their careers on Astroturf. Grass is real and had to be a favorite of mine. Turf is good for those quick fast guys, you know, but it's still bad for you.

In your contract days, what were your lowest and highest salaries?

Oh man, people have a hard time realizing that coming out in 1986, as a second round draft choice, you get a contract of about $18,500 and a signing bonus of about $25,000. Things really got going good when I was getting out, so I came out at about $300,000.

What is your favorite Viking game and why?

The first one has got to be the Super Bowl. Win or lose, you know, just to play in the Super Bowl and get that kind of experience is unbelievable. But, leading up to the Super Bowl, we had some good games against Detroit and some good games against the Bears, and each team were rivals in the league. You know, if you do good against those guys, you just feel special. The fans will always be on your side and will love you to death for when you do have those kinds of games.

How many autographs do you think you've signed over the years?

That's tough to put a finger on. If it's not a million, I'm real close.

What are your thoughts on playing the game today and playing the game yesterday?

There's a big difference today, you know. You look at the game like you're watching a variety show or something, because everybody has something to bring to the game. And the days when we played the game, we brought to the game the love and passion and just wanted to play the game. We didn't want to be seen; we just wanted to do our job and help our team win.

Being a wide receiver, who do you think is the best wide receiver in the game today?

Whoa! You know, I love Randy Moss. He got real this year, but you know, off the field he doesn't measure up to what he does on the field. Still my favorite is Randy Moss. But my all-time favorite is Jerry Rice.

What would you say to kids today who are playing in sports?

You know, you got to pay a price at any level. The high school, junior high, college, pros, you know, you gotta pay the price. You gotta put your time in on the field, off the field, you gotta do your books. It's too tough these days to play any sport if you don't come up with a certain grade point average and pass so many courses. So you got to do these things. And you always got to know who's in charge. Always respect your parents, coaches, you know, and your elders.

#81 NATE BURLESON

WIDE RECEIVER 2003-PRESENT

Photo taken 2005

STATS

HIGH SCHOOL
Name of School: O' Dea High School
Location of School: Seattle, Washington
Graduation Year: 1999
Position: Wide Receiver
Jersey number: 13
Height: 6 feet 1 inch
Weight: 165 pounds
40 speed: 4.6 seconds
Coach: Mante Kohler
Other sports played: Track and basketball

COLLEGE
Name of School: Nevada-Reno
Location of School: Reno, Nevada
Final year: 2003
How long attended: Four years
Did you graduate? No
Major: Human Development and Family
    Studies
Position: Wide Receiver
Jersey number: 80
Height: 6 feet 1 inch
Weight: 195 pounds
40 speed: 4.3 seconds
Other sports played: None

PRO
Position: Wide Receiver
Jersey number: 81
Year Drafted: 2003
Draft Round: Third
Height: 6 feet 1 inch
Weight: 195 pounds
40 speed: 4.3 seconds
Coach: Mike Tice

When did you first get into football?

I started playing football when I was eight years old. My dad wanted me to play and it seemed like the best thing because all my friends were playing at the time.

What position did you play?

When I was little, I actually played defensive end and tight end. I wasn't fast, I was just long and lanky. So they put me on the end of the line of scrimmage.

How many brothers and sisters do you have?

I have two older brothers and one younger brother, so four boys.

Are you the only one who went into the professional ranks?

Yeah. Well, my dad played professional and my older brother, Kevin Burleson, plays basketball overseas professionally.

What team did your dad play for?

He got picked up by the New Orleans Saints and then played nine years in the Canadian Football League.

What position?

Safety.

Did you play any other sports in high school?

Track and basketball.

What was your best game in college?

I played against San Jose State, and I had twelve catches for 326 yards. At that point I felt I was pretty unstoppable in my conference. I knew there was a lot more talent out there, but as far as the WAC Conference I was playing in, I didn't think anybody could stop me.

When you were drafted with the Vikings, what did you think knowing that Randy Moss was on the team and other people were on the team when you were drafted here?
It was tough because coming out of college I was "the man" but coming here I knew I would be a sidekick to one of the best players to ever play the game.

The 2004 season was your breakout season, how did you feel about the play?
I think I did pretty good. I stepped up and made some things happen, but at the same time I made some mistakes. So it's always a good thing knowing you can get better.

How do you prepare yourself for this coming season so you don't make those same mistakes?
You have to just study the film and determine what you can improve on and take your attributes and continue to do better.

What do you look for in the film to better yourself?
You've got to watch every little thing about your play. You have to watch everything from your hand placement to your footwork, the explosion off the ball and how good you read the defense on the fly. You have to break down everything, it's not just about the simple things like how fast you can run and how you catch the ball. It's more than that when it comes to professional sports. You have to watch certain things with your hands or you do certain things with your feet and how you line up that will tip off the defense. So, you got to know what things you do to give away your routes. And the professionals here can take advantage of your weaknesses and use them against you.

What advice do you have for kids about sports and education?
I'd just say stick with it because there are a lot of athletes who might be better than you, who get more publicity, more exposure, but the ones who stick with it the longest are usually the ones with

long careers. I never thought I'd be in the NFL, and I can name a whole handful of guys who are better than me at each level I played at but I just continued to stick with it. This is my craft. This is my job. This is what God placed me on this earth to do.

#18   RYAN HOAG

WIDE RECEIVER   2003-PRESENT

Photo taken 2005

STATS

HIGH SCHOOL

Name of School: Minneapolis Washburn
Location of School: Minneapolis,
    Minnesota
Graduation Year: 1998
Position: Quarterback one year but
    soccer most my life
Height: 5 feet 11 inches
Weight: 165 pounds
Coach: Coach Haugen
Other sports played: Tennis, basketball
    soccer

COLLEGE

Name of School: Gustavus Adolphus
    College
Location of School: St. Peter, Minnesota
Graduation Year: 2003
How long attended: 4 years
Did you graduate? Yes
Degree: Elementary Education
Position: Wide Receiver and Kick-Off Return
Jersey number: 2
Height: 6 feet 2 inches
Weight: 185 pounds
40 speed: 4.33 seconds
Coach: Coach Schoenebeck
Other sports played: Track

PRO

Position: Wide Receiver and Kick-Off
    Return
Jersey number: 18
Year Drafted: 2003
Draft Round: Seventh
Height: 6 feet 3 inches
Weight: 200 pounds
40 speed: 4.4 seconds
Coach: Mike Tice

What University did you graduate from?
Gustavas Adolphus College

How many years have you been in the pros?
I'm entering my third year.

Were you always with the Vikings?
I was drafted by the Raiders, which is irrelevant. Then I played
with the Giants, then with the Vikings last year.

How do you juggle your family life and your career?
Well, I'm not married. I'm single. I'm from the area, so obviously
it's great to be home as opposed to the east and west coasts. It's fun
that my family gets to see me play live and obviously it's important
for them to see me succeed in whatever I do, but I have other
career plans if this doesn't pan out.

Did you have any mentor or coaches who guided you through your career?
Definitely my wide receiver coach in college, Tom Brown. He was
in a couple NFL camps and he nurtured me. Also a guy named
Steve Rosker. He's a local guy and was my trainer throughout college. Even now he does a little bit of training with me, and he's
given me the heads-up on what to expect.

Do you have any goals for your upcoming year, 2005?
My goal is to be the number-one special teams player on the team.
I want to stand out, I want to be a top-five return guy. I want to
lead the league as a kick-off return guy. I think that's doable. I definitely want to take a leadership role on the special teams.

Have you had any injuries over the years?

I was released by the Giants because I tore a ligament in my hand. And then I was put on IR [Injured Reserve] the last couple weeks of last year because I separated my SC [Sternoclavicular] joint in my shoulder.

You mentioned you have other career plans if this doesn't pan out.

Yeah, I'm an elementary education major. My plan is to teach first grade whenever my NFL career comes to an end.

What's your fastest time in the 40?

4.33 seconds my junior year.

The Vikings have never had a special teams guy who can return punts or kicks. Do you think you can fill that job?

Absolutely. That's really going to be my niche and I had a meeting with coach Tice this off-season and gave him my vision. He was right alongside where I'm at so I'm excited about that.

#83   STU VOIGT

TIGHT END   1970-1980

Photo taken 1976

STATS

HIGH SCHOOL
Name of School: Madison West High School
Location of School: Madison, Wisconsin
Graduation Year: June 1965
Position: Halfback
Jersey number: 28
Height: 6 feet 1 1/2 inches
Weight: 220 pounds
40 speed: 4.8 seconds
Coach: Burt Hable
Other sports played: Baseball, track

COLLEGE
Name of School: University of Wisconsin
Location of School: Madison, Wisconsin
Graduation Year: 1970
How long attended: 7 years
Did you graduate? Yes. BBA 1970, MBA 1973
Degree: BBA and MBA in Finance
Position: Fullback and Tight End
Jersey number: 40
Height: 6 feet 2 inches
Weight: 225 pounds
40 speed: 4.8 seconds
Coach: John Coatta
Other sports played: Track, baseball

PRO
Position: Tight end
Jersey number: 83
Year Drafted: 1970
Draft Round: Tenth
Year Retired: after 1980—11 years
Height: 6 feet 2 inches
Weight: 230 pounds
40 speed: 4.8 seconds
Coach: Bud Grant

Stu Voigt played eleven seasons with the Minnesota Vikings. He started in three Super Bowls and finished his career as the Vikings leading tight end receiver, holding records in yardage, receptions, and touchdowns. He was also a premier blocking tight end. In 1985, Voigt was named a member of the Vikings All-Time Team.

Stu had an illustrious career at the University of Wisconsin where he lettered in football, baseball, and track. He was Wisconsin's MVP in football in 1969 and is the Big Ten's last three-sport letterman. Voigt was inducted into Wisconsin's Hall of Fame in 1999. He received his BBA and MBA from the University of Wisconsin where he majored in management.

Stu is currently the president of Ramco, a real estate development firm in Minneapolis. He also works as a color commentator on Vikings Football broadcasts on WCCO, the CBS affiliate in Minneapolis. Voigt also serves as Chairman of the Board of both First Commercial Bank and Assured Financial LLC in the Twin Cities and as director of Bank Vista in Sartell, Minnesota. Stu and his wife, Linda, currently live in Apple Valley, Minnesota.

How did you earn your nickname "Chainsaw?"
In the 1970s, the Vikings main rival was the Rams. They had a player named "Hacksaw" Jack Reynolds, a middle linebacker, who I had to block quite a bit. Fran Tarkenton came up with the nickname. To go against "Hacksaw," the Vikings would use a "Chainsaw." The nickname stuck even though our rivalry was diminished in the years to come.

What was your job in the off-season?
After completing my MBA in finance in 1973, I started my real estate business, which involves commercial development. Recently, I have branched out into banking where I am involved in the ownership of two banks in the Twin Cities area.

What was your rookie year salary, bonus, etc.?
My rookie salary in 1970 was $15,000 with a $7,500 signing bonus.

#83   STEVE JORDAN

TIGHT END   1982-1994

Photo taken 1991

STATS

HIGH SCHOOL
Name of School: South Mountain High
    School
Location of School: Phoenix, Arizona
Graduation Year: 1978
Position: Quarterback, Tight End
Jersey number: 13
Height: 6 feet 2 inches
Weight: 195 pounds
Coach: Earl Clapper
Other sports played: Tennis, basketball

COLLEGE
Name of School: Brown University
Location of School: Providence, Rhode Island
Graduation Year: 1982
How long attended: Four years
Did you graduate? Yes
Degree: B.S. in Civil Engineering
Position: Tight End
Jersey number: 85
Height: 6 feet 4 inches
Weight: 230 pounds
40 speed: 4.7 seconds
Coach: John Anderson
Other sports played: None

PRO
Position: Tight End
Jersey number: 83
Year Drafted: 1982
Draft Round: Seventh
Year Retired: 1995
Height: 6 feet 4 inches
Weight: 245 pounds
40 speed: 4.7 seconds
Coach: Bud Grant, Les Steckel, Jerry
    Burns, Dennis Green

What are your likes and dislikes of signing autographs?

Likes: Making a person smile and the opportunity to talk to people, especially the kids.

Dislikes: Rude people who think you owe them an autograph—no matter where you are or what the circumstances are. Inconsiderate people/kids who don't even say thank you.

What are your likes and dislikes of media attention?

Likes: The ability to convey information to which the fans can relate.

Dislikes: The inconsiderate behavior of media people just to get a quote or a story. I also don't like how sometimes the story will be manipulated by the media resulting in inaccurate information being printed in the story.

What is your pre-game routine?

My routine was simple and efficient. My ankles were taped at the hotel. I would do a final review of any last minute changes on the bus ride to the stadium. I wasn't one of those guys who liked to get to the stadium early—just in time was fine for me. I would get dressed, go eat with the team for warm ups. We'd come back in for last-minute adjustments, I'd say a prayer for safety for all, performance, and glorification of him.

#85 JERMAINE WIGGINS

TIGHT END 2004-PRESENT

Photo taken 2005

STATS

HIGH SCHOOL
Name of School: East Boston
Location of School: Boston, Massachusetts
Graduation Year: 1993
Position: Quarterback
Jersey number: 18
Height: 6 feet 2 inches
Weight: 220 pounds
Coach: Coach Loftuis
Other sports played: Basketball

COLLEGE
Name of School: Marshall (2 years), Georgia (2 years)
Location of Schools: Huntington, West Virginia, and Athens, Georgia
Graduation Year: 1998
How long attended: Four years
Did you graduate? Yes
Degree: Child Family Development
Position: Tight End
Jersey number: 89
Height: 6 feet 3 inches
Weight: 250 pounds
40 speed: 4.8 seconds
Coach: Jim Donnan
Other sports played: None

PRO
Position: Tight End
Jersey number: 85
Free Agent/Other: Rookie
Height: 6 feet 3 inches
Weight: 255 pounds
Coach: Mike Tice

When did you start thinking of getting into football?

I always played sports. I grew up in a city where the Boys Club was a way to get away from doing the wrong thing and staying off the streets, so we played every sport we could think of.

The city where you grew up, were there any other players that made it to the pros like you?

The only other guy that made it from the metro area of Boston was Ron Stone. He was the only other guy.

Were you big for your age growing up?

I was a basketball player—that was my big thing, but I never thought I was going to make it at a pro level. I think every kid has dreams about that kind of thing, but I was 6 feet 2 inches. Powerful, but I played more out of enjoyment. I was looking more to get into college on a partial scholarship or a scholarship to a small school. Football was something I enjoyed doing but I never had any big aspirations about playing in the pros or anything like that.

When you went to college, did you feel you might have a chance to become a pro?

I went to Marshall my first two years and back then—pre-Randy Moss—there weren't too many guys that made it out of Marshall. It was the number one AA school at that time, but no one really got drafted. There were a couple guys that made it to free agency—Troy Brown, Mike Bochum—but I didn't really think about it. I didn't have anybody in front of me who had done it except for Troy.

What team did you try out for as a free agent?

The first team was the New York Jets in '99, this was [Bill] Parcell's second year there or something to that effect. It was a good experience for me back then. I had the opportunity to learn from a lot of wise and experienced veterans—not only the guys who were in my position, but all the guys who were on the team. I played with guys like Erik Green, Steve Atwater, Keith Byars, Vinnie Testaverde, Richie Anderson. A lot of those guys just showed me what the pros were all about—what it takes to make it to the next level.

Did you have a chance to play in your first year there?

No, the first year, I got cut the last game of the pre-season. I was out for a couple weeks, and then Bill [Belichick] brought me back, and I was on practice squad, then got cut again, and then came back again. So I ended up probably getting about eleven weeks total of practice squad my first year. It was definitely a great experience for me because it gave me the standpoint of the guys who weren't drafted, and knowing what it's like being on the streets. So definitely, I matured a lot quicker coming up the way I did.

Where did your career take you after New York?

I was in New York for about two years. My second year I played a little bit, like the third tight end, special teams, that kind of thing. I was released at week twelve, basically to be put on practice squad so they could bring another guy in to make the roster solid. Bill Belichick took the head coaching job in New England, and I knew Bill from the year previous from being on practice squad. He gave me a shot in New England and the next week was my first real taste of the NFL. I was cut from New York on a Tuesday and the following Monday I was playing on Monday Night Football with New England. I had five catches and a touchdown my first game out and did some really good things my last four games of the season with

New England. Obviously, the next year we went to the Super Bowl, which was definitely a tremendous route for me and a great experience.

How was the road to the Super Bowl different for New England that year?

Obviously, you come off the year we did before we went—we were 5 and 11—so the expectations of the team were really not high. Maybe we'd get to 8 wins or something like that. I don't think anyone was really expecting us to do what we did, but midway through the season we were probably 5 and 5 when we hit that point where we just ran the table and ended up being 11 and 5. [Tom] Brady came in and did a tremendous job, and the guys on the team were tremendous players. We had a few super stars but most of the guys were just hard-working guys who didn't make mistakes and took pride in doing their job. We had a team of good veteran leadership, and we went on a good run, went on and beat Oakland, went and beat Pittsburgh, and then beat St. Louis in the Super Bowl. We were the underdog in the games, and no one expected us to do anything but the guys in that locker room, so I think that was the big factor as to why we had so much success.

How did it feel after winning the Super Bowl?

It was kind of a crazy feeling. I grew up in Boston, and we take pride in all our hometown teams. So to grow up in Boston, and play in New England and win a Super Bowl for New England is something you can't imagine. Most guys say a dream would be to play in a Super Bowl, and that's everybody's, but if you were to ask a guy, what would be the ultimate goal, the ultimate dream, you know, 100 percent of us would be to play in a Super Bowl for our hometown team that we grew up watching as kids.

Do you have your Super Bowl ring locked away or do you wear it all the time?

Yeah, I wear it. I'm not one of those guys who locks it away. I wear it for special occasions, I wear it often. I figure, hey, I worked my butt off to get this thing, I'm going to wear it as much as I can. That's just my take on it.

What was the road like to get to the Vikings?

After that I bounced around. I went to Indy for a short stint, then Carolina, I picked up with them in 2002-2003 and had a chance to go back to the Super Bowl and experience it again and from a losing side, so after that, I had the opportunity to come here. Coach Tice was up front by saying, "Hey, you can come in here. We know what you can do and we're going to give you the opportunity to do what you know you can do and that's to make a lot of big plays." If you look at my track record, prior to when I got here, I didn't a have bunch of numbers, but my plays stand out. It's been a great career for me. It's definitely been a hard career, it's not been a cake walk like some guys, but there have been other guys that came up the same way I came up, some even in a harder way. So you know, I wouldn't change a thing about it.

Last year, you were a steady player for the Vikings. You lead the team in receptions. Did you ever think you'd lead a team in receptions?

No, I never thought I'd lead a team in receptions. I'm not going to say that I don't feel like I have the skills to do that, I know I have the skills to put up 50, 60, 70 catches a year, but I never thought that I'd lead a team. But it's not just me. Daunte does a great job and the players around us do a great job, the coaching staff does a great job of putting us in a position to make great plays. I just had the opportunity to go out there and make plays and it worked out that way for me. When you come up like me, an undrafted rookie, free agent, you don't expect a lot. You just want to play as long as you can in the NFL and just be on a roster year in and year out. We don't think about those Pro Bowls and Super Bowls, and leading teams in receptions because guys like us feel like it's all about making the team year in, year out. Obviously we know that we can do those kinds of things given the opportunity, but like I said, when you're a rookie free agent, you don't get the same opportunity as draft picks, so it's tough to do those types of things.

When your career is completed, what will you take from the game?

I definitely will take a lot of knowledge from the game, from a business standpoint. Yes, it's a game but it's still looked at as a business in that you can't play this game thinking that everything will be peaches and cream. You have to look at it from a reality standpoint of the game, you have to go out there week in and week out and prove to everybody that you deserve to be in this league.

I can also say I had the ability to play with future Hall of Famer, Daunte Culpepper, or a guy like Tom Brady or Randy Moss. I'll be able to tell my kids, my grandkids, that I had the opportunity to play with those guys. You know, maybe even the guys who weren't Hall of Famers who are true pros, guys like a Rodney Peete, Rickey Proehl and have those friendships and bonds that you've grown over the years. I think that's the biggest thing for me that I look at after the game is over.

What's your favorite food?

Chicken parmesan. I'm Italian. My mother's Italian, my grand-mother's Italian . . .

What message do you have for the kids who have aspirations of playing football?

My message I give to a lot of the youths now is that, regardless of what they say, don't let them shatter your dreams. Because someone is always going to say, well, you can't do this or you can't do that. You've got to know that you can. Even if you face some adversity, know that anything's possible. Look what I've done.

What's your favorite charity?

The Boys and Girls Club of Boston and America in general.

#78 MATT BIRK

OFFENSIVE LINE 1998-PRESENT

Photo taken 2005

S T A T S

HIGH SCHOOL
Name of School: Cretin-Derham Hall
Location of School: St. Paul, Minnesota
Graduation Year: 1994
Position: Defensive End
Jersey number: 75
Height: 6 feet 4 inches
Weight: 230 pounds
Coach: Coach Kallok, Coach Scanlon
Other sports played: Basketball

COLLEGE
Name of School: Harvard
Location of School: Cambridge,
    Massachusetts
Graduation Year: 1998
How long attended: Four years
Did you graduate? Yes
Degree: Economics
Position: Offensive Tackle
Jersey number: 50
Height: 6 feet 5 inches
Weight: 300 pounds
Coach: Coach Murphy
Other sports played: None

PRO
Position: Center
Jersey number: 78
Year Drafted: 1998
Draft Round: Sixth
Height: 6 feet 5 inches
Weight: 300 pounds
Coach: Dennis Green, Mike Tice

What round were you drafted?
Sixth round, 1998.

When you first got here, who were the centers?
Jeff Christy was the starting center, and Everett Lindsay was the backup.

Did they help you learn your position?
Oh, no question. I never played center before I got here, so Jeff was a Pro-Bowler and a very smart player and it was good to learn under a guy like that for a couple years to see how he approached the position. It's always good to learn from the best.

Can you name some of your teammates who made it that year with you as a rookie?
Randy Moss, Kailee Wong—that might be about it.

Did you have a chance to start or play at all as a rookie?
I actually got in for some significant play time, actually the last game of the year due to injury. But other than that, I was pretty much inactive for the first half and after that, the second half I would get some mop-up duty at the end of some of the games.

What was the hardest part of training camp for you as a rookie?
Just the whole overall experience. The level of talent was much greater than I was used to in college. Just kind of getting used to that and a new offense and new teammates. Everything is new and everything just kind of hits you at once. It can be overwhelming. You've just got to remember to take deep breaths and just take it one step at a time.

Were there any other players who made it to the NFL from Harvard who went on further than you?

No. There's one other guy who was a teammate of mine who is playing in the league right now with Seattle—special teams and backing up. But there is a lot of talent at Harvard and in the Ivy League; it's just finding the right situation and the place where you can latch on.

Being what Harvard is known for, did you think you'd have the success that you're having right now by going there?

No, I never did. I never really focused on results. I focused more on making sure that I put forth maximum effort and gave it my all. I'm as surprised as anybody that I've stuck around this long and have been able to play on so many good teams. To do that, you definitely work hard in the off-season.

#73 ADAM GOLDBERG

OFFENSIVE LINE 2003-PRESENT

Photo taken 2005

STATS

HIGH SCHOOL
Name of School: Edina High School
Location of School: Edina, Minnesota
Graduation Year: 1998
Position: Offensive Tackle and Defensive
    End
Jersey number: 75
Height: 6 feet 5 inches
Weight: 275 pounds
40 speed: 4.9 seconds
Coach: Todd Olson
Other sports played: Basketball

COLLEGE
Name of School: University of Wyoming
Location of School: Laramie, Wyoming
Graduation Year: 2003
How long attended: Five years
Did you graduate? Yes
Degree: Finance and English
Position: Offensive Tackle
Jersey number: 74
Height: 6 feet 6 inches
Weight: 315 pounds
40 speed: 5.07 seconds
Coach: Dana Dimel and Vic Koening
Other sports played: None

PRO
Position: Offensive Line
Jersey number: 73
Year Drafted: 2003
Free Agent/Other: Free Agent
Height: 6 feet 6 inches
Weight: 325 pounds
40 speed: 5.07 seconds
Coach: Mike Tice

When did you start getting into the game of football?

In high school. I played youth football as well, but it was always secondary behind basketball.

What position did you play?

Defensive end and offensive tackle.

Was your family part of your play growing up?

Yeah, they were. They never coached or anything, but they were always really supportive and went to the games and made sure I was there before I had my driver's license and things like that.

Was there any other player in high school who went into college and professional as you did?

Mike Lehan from Hopkins is still in the league.

At what age did you start training and getting into weights?

A freshman in college. I never lifted weights in high school. I just played basketball.

What position on the basketball team did you play?

Forward.

So from basketball, you went into football as a walk-on at the University of Minnesota?

No. I was at the University of Wyoming. I was a scholarship player there. I was offensive tackle.

Were you a free agent or drafted for the Vikings?

I was a free agent. They called me in the middle of the seventh round and said that if I made it through and didn't get picked up, they were interested in me as free agency. There were about five or six teams in a bidding war right after the draft, and the Vikings won.

2004 was a great season for you. How did that impact you as a player?

It was a big year for me. Unfortunately, when you're a back-up, it's a tough situation because you only get your chance to play when something bad happens to one of the guys in front of you, and then Mike Rosenthal got hurt, right tackle got hurt and then they put me in. They liked what I was doing, so they kept me in for the rest of the year. It was a great experience.

What more do you need to do to be a starter for the Vikings?

I think the most important thing is having a solid work ethic and not letting anyone outwork you. There are a lot of talented people in the league. There are a lot of big people, a lot of strong people, a lot of fast people, but what separates people is their work ethic and how professional they are and how they go about their job.

What advice do you have for kids on sports and education?

Just take the lessons you learned in sports and apply them into all the avenues of your life and what you are working on currently.

#53 MICK TINGELHOFF

CENTER   1962-1978

Photo taken 2001

STATS

HIGH SCHOOL
Name of School: Lexington High School
Location of School: Lexington, Nebraska
Graduation Year: 1958
Position: Center and Linebacker
Number: 77
Height: 6 feet 1 inch
Weight: 175 pounds
Coach: Merle Applebee

COLLEGE
Name of School: University of Nebraska
Location of School: Lincoln, Nebraska
Graduation Year: 1962
How long attended: 4 years
Position: Center and Linebacker
Number: 51
Height: 6 feet 1 inch
Weight: 210 pounds
Coach: Bill Jennings

PRO
Position: Center
Number: 53
Free Agent/Other: 1962
Year Retired: 1978
Height: 6 feet 2 inches
Weight: 270 pounds
Coaches: Norm Van Brocklin,
    Bud Grant

Was your size for a center back when you played considered big or small?

I was probably in the middle somewhere. I wasn't real, real big or real, real small. I played at 250-260 and ended up around 270 and about 6 feet 2 inches.

Did any of your teammates from the University of Nebraska make the NFL along with you that year?

Pat Fischer was the defensive back for the St. Louis Cardinals and Roland McDole was the offensive tackle of the St. Louis Cardinals. They were in my class at Nebraska.

How much was your signing bonus?

I did not get a signing bonus.

What was your biggest contract amount in one year?

I think I made $190,000 as my biggest amount in the '70s.

Before you were a Viking, did you have a favorite NFL team? Did you follow the Vikings at all prior to becoming one?

Not really. I grew up in Nebraska and went to the University of Nebraska and, to tell you the truth, I really didn't watch pro football that much. I was busy studying and all that stuff [laughter].

Do you think your NFL Pension helps you today?

Yeah. It's not a whole lot, but I like it, so my wife takes it anyway.

What year(s) do you consider to have been the best for the Vikings offensive line? Could you name some of the players at that time?

Oh, we had a really good line in the '70's there. We went to several Super Bowls with Ed White and Milt Sunde, Grady Alderman and Ron Yary. We had a pretty good offensive line.

What was the coldest day for you playing at the Met?

I don't remember for sure but it was well below zero. I think it was twenty below zero or something like that.

What team were you playing at the time?

I know we had a couple of really cold games against the Chicago Bears and then we had a couple cold ones with the Packers, too.

Why did most of the Vikings live in Lakeville when you played?

We just moved out here, and why? I have no idea. There are several that are still here, today. There's [Dave] Osborn, [Bob] Lurtsema, Wally Hilgenberg, and myself still live within two or three miles of each other.

Who was your best friend on the team when you played?

Oh gosh, I had a lot of them, really. It was hard to say who was my best friend, we had a really close team. Of course, Fran Tarkenton is still a close friend of mine. All the guys were real close. Dave Osborn, Bill Brown, Jim Marshall, of course, [Carl] Eller. We were a real close team.

How difficult is it today to think about and relive, some 20-plus years later, having not won a Super Bowl?
I played in all four of them, and it's just one of those things. We played well, we were well prepared and everything, but we just didn't win. Somebody's got to lose, somebody's got to win, and why? I'll never know. We beat the teams before and during the season but on that given day we just didn't play well enough to win.

It is the opinion of many former players and fans that you should be in the Hall of Fame. Do you feel you deserve a placement?
Yeah, I guess I do because of the record I had—240 straight games or something like that. I played seventeen years and was All-Pro several times. So yeah, I think I should.

What were some of the fun things about playing for the Vikings?
I think it was all about the players I played with and the friendships we made. You know, it's been a long time since I played and I still know all the players I played with. They are still good buddies. I think that's the real joy of playing with my teammates. They're awesome guys and still close friends.

Do you think that's something unique to the Vikings or did other teams experience the same thing, too?
I think other teams did that, too, but it just seems like when I see Matt [Blair] or I see Carl Eller or [Jim] Marshall or whatever, it's something special to have played with those great kind of people.

Did you have a job in the off-season? What was it?

I did work a little bit as a stockbroker. I got my license as a stock-broker with a company here. I always liked the stock market.

Did you do that while you were still playing?

Yes. I got my license and then, when I retired, I didn't follow up on it very much.

Who was your roommate at Training Camp?

Fran [Tarkenton] and I roomed together, you know, and we came out to be good friends. I don't have any big stories, or anything special. We were roommates together for several years.

1976. NFC Championship Game against the Redskins. Calvin Hill goes across the middle for a pass and I smack him. The hit was so intense that my helmet comes off and he goes down hard. Fred [Zambreletti] comes out to assist me off the field because I lost my tooth. I had a slight concussion and had to stay overnight at the local hospital for observation. We go on to win the game. Wednesday we go back to practice to loosen up in preparing to play the Oakland Raiders in Super Bowl XI. The offense is running their plays and then you bend down, and . . .

I bent down and found your tooth. Boy, that was a long time ago.

Did you still have aspirations to play in the NFL?

Oh yeah! I wanted to play. I'd say if I watched anybody it was the St. Louis Cardinals. I had a couple teammates out of Nebraska play for St. Louis: Pat Fischer, Roland McDole. I was watching them and learned how to get there and do it.

Do you still follow the team today?

Oh, yeah. I read about them all the time. I was just reading about Matt Birk. I don't know much about the injury, but I'm sure the trainers there have it under control. I wish him the best and I hope everything works out for him. I really am a fan. I enjoyed the game and I was fortunate I got to play a long time. I was injury free which was pretty fortunate and lucky, you know. My old career was pretty good. I enjoyed it. It was a lot of fun.

#76   TIM IRWIN

TACKLE   1981-1993

Photo taken 2001

STATS

HIGH SCHOOL
Name of School: Central High School
Location of School: Knoxville, Tennesse
Graduation Year: 1976
Position: Tight End and Nose Guard
Number: 77
Height: 6 feet 6 inches
Weight: 245 pounds
Coach: Tom Schumpert
Other sports played: Basketball and tra

COLLEGE
Name of School: University of Tennessee
Location of School: Knoxville, Tennessee
Graduation Year: 1980
How long attended: Four years
Did you graduate? Yes
Degree: Honors in Political Science
Position: Tackle
Number: 78
Height: 6 feet 6 inches
Weight: 245 pounds
40 speed: 5.1 seconds
Coach: John Majors
Other sports played: None

PRO
Position: Tackle
Number: 76
Year Drafted: 1981
Draft Round: Third
Year Retired: 1993
Height: 6 feet 7 inches
Weight: 297 pounds
40 speed: 5.1 seconds
Coach : Bud Grant, Les Steckel,
     Jerry Burns

In the early years of college, did you think you'd be playing in the NFL?

No.

What makes an NFL player, like yourself, play as long as you did and be successful?

Being born 6 feet 7 inches, working hard in the weight room, having John Michaels for a coach, and having a fear of failure.

What was going through you mind before a game?

Getting off on the snap every play and totally selling out. Making sure there was nothing left in the tank at the end.

Did you watch film the week of practice prior to the game without the coaches?

Yes, for about two to three hours per week.

What was the biggest joke either during training camp or during the season?

The biggest joke was always the "Free Turkey." But one time, Kirk Lowdermilk told Brian Habib that John Madden wanted to interview him before a big game. Brian walked around all day wondering what he was going to say, and of course, it was all just a joke.

Did you win any contest during training camp?

I won Best Singer.

What was the hardest thing about training camp?

The boredom.

How difficult was it to make the team?

Extremely difficult as a new player on a Bud Grant team.

Did you set any goals while you were in the NFL?
Yes, my goal was to start 100 games in a row. I actually started 197 in a row.

What is your current job?
I'm an attorney and a sports agent.

Tell the readers what your lowest and highest season contracts were.
$30,000.00 was my lowest, and $950,000.00 was my highest.

Who was your best friend on the team?
Wade Wilson.

If you needed a football question answered, who would you ask?
John Michaels.

What did you get out of playing in the NFL?
Financial security, a competitive edge, and a sense of pride and accomplishment along with a lot of lifelong friends and fans.

What does it take to be a Viking?
Size, speed, strength, agility, and a will not to be beaten.

What was your best game as a Viking?
The 1988 NFC Championship loss to Washington. I held All-Pro Charles Mann to half a tackle and no sacks.

How do you feel about the NFL retirement package?
Increases need to continue to be bargained for by the Union.

What is your favorite food?
My mother's lasagna.

How did family fit into the role of your career? Who took precedence?
Definitely, family first.

What can you say to kids about sports?
Have fun! Learn to love the game you choose.

Can you say four things about the importance of education?
1) Paramount
2) Sports don't last forever
3) Knowledge is the key to power and understanding
4) Reading is the key to knowledge

What would you say to your fans out there?
I have heard every cheer and every boo, and I always appreciated you, and I miss you. My thirteen years with the Vikings were great.

#64 RANDALL MCDANIEL

OFFENSIVE LINE   1988-1999

Photo courtesy of Rick Kolodziel

S T A T S

HIGH SCHOOL
Name of School: Agua Fria High School
Location of School: Avondale, Arizona
Graduation: 1983
Position: Tight end, Offensive Lineback
Number: 88
Height: 6 foot 3 inches
Weight: 225 Pounds
40 speed: 4.6 Seconds
Coach: Pat Levin
Other sports played: Basketball and tra
   (shot, disc, 10M, 200M, 4x100 relay a
   mile relay)

COLLEGE
Name of School: Arizona State University
Location of School: Tempe, Arizona
Graduation Year: 1988
How long attended: 5 years
Did you graduate? Yes, in 1990
Degree: Bachelor of Science and Physical
   Education
Position: Tight End (1 year), Offensive Guard
   (4 years)
Number: 62
Height: 6 feet 4 inches
Weight: 235-265 pounds
40 speed: 4.58 seconds
Coach: Daryl Rogers, John Cooper
Other sports played: None

PRO
Position: Offensive Guard
Number: 64
Year Drafted: 1988
Draft Round: First
Year Retired: 2002
Height: 6 feet 4 inches
Weight: 280 pounds
40 speed: 4.5 seconds
Coach: Jerry Burns, Dennis Green,
   Tony Dungy

What is the thrill/glory of being an offensive guard?

The life of an offensive lineman is different than most positions on the team. We are the "blue collar" workers—we just go out and do our job without much glory or fanfare. The thrill comes through personal satisfaction of doing your job well. When the line works flawlessly and allows the running back or the quarterback to do their job, you feel a sense of accomplishment. Offensive linemen have a unique connection. We are the only players on the team who are completely dependent on each other to reach our goals. There is no room for personal glory—you succeed or fail as a group. We knew that the success of the offense depended on us. The thrill, for me, was trying to live up to that challenge.

Did you prepare to work after football? What did you do?

After my football career, I had always envisioned working with children. I already had earned my degree in physical education from Arizona State and originally thought I would become a PE teacher. Playing professional football gave me the opportunity to work with many children in the community. The focus of my programs was education. My wife and I created an after-school program with the YWCA Transitional Housing Program. This program used multicultural activities to encourage learning in a nurturing environment. We also developed an educational "pilot program" in the St. Louis Area. This program used outdoor adventure and experiential education with "at-risk" youth to develop leadership skills. In Tampa, we developed "Mr. McDaniel's Classroom" in conjunction with the Children's Cancer Center. This after-school program provides children with sickle cell anemia the opportunity to work one-on-one with a volunteer tutor to "catch-up" on school work missed due to frequent hospitalizations. My experiences with these programs led me to decide to teach elementary school. In 1996, I began volunteering in the Robbinsdale District as a teacher's aide in my "off seasons." When I retired in 2002, I obtained a teaching license and began substitute teaching in Robbinsdale. I am currently attending Hamline University to receive a post-baccalaureate degree in teaching education. After completing the program, I hope to receive a permanent teaching license and become a third- or fourth-grade teacher.

How did the Viking fans treat you?

Viking fans were always good to me. I was continually amazed how much they supported and believed in the team. I have always believed the fans are the reason athletes are afforded the opportunities that we have. Because of this, I felt it was important to give back to the community and be accessible to the fans. I enjoyed the chance to interact with fans and show them I was a "regular guy." I think it's very important for athletes to keep everything in perspective. Athletes are given a certain status by the community and I believe that is a responsibility we need to take very seriously. I know I do.

THE DEFENSE/
SPECIAL TEAMS

#70   JIM MARSHALL

DEFENSIVE LINE   1961-1979

Photo taken 1975

S T A T S

HIGH SCHOOL
Name of School: Columbus East High School
Location of School: Columbus, Ohio
Graduation year: 1956
Position: Offensive, Defensive Tackle, Tight End, Running Back, Linebacke
Jersey number: 7
Height: 6 feet 3 inches
Weight: 185 pounds
Coach: Coach Ralph Webster
Other sports played: Track and field

COLLEGE
Name of School: Ohio State University
Location of School: Columbus, Ohio
Did you graduate? Not at that time
Degree: Education (I went back to get my degree)
Position: Offensvie Tackle, Defensive Tackle
Jersey number: 76
Height: 6 feet 4 inches
Weight: 220 pounds
40 speed: 4.45 seconds
Coach: Woody Hayes
Other sports played: Track

PRO
Position: Defensive End
Jersey number: 70
Year Drafted: 1959 by the Cleveland Browns, but I chose to go to Canada so I chose to come back to play with the Cleveland Browns in 1960 and matriculated to the Minnesota Viking in 1961
Year Retired: 1979
Height: 6 feet 4 inches
Weight: 220 pounds
40 speed: 4.45 seconds
Coaches: Norm Van Brocklin, Bud Gra

How did you manage to last twenty years in the NFL?

I just loved the game. I played football so long because I had a lot of luck. I didn't have injuries—well, not crippling injuries, anyway.

Mentally, how did you keep yourself together for twenty years?

I felt I had an obligation to do a job that I'd been hired to do, and I had fun doing it. I never thought about how long I was playing. I just loved playing and, as long as it was fun for me, I played.

Was your first training camp with the Vikings or was it some-place else?

My first training camp was actually with the Saskatchewan Roughriders in the Canadian Football League. It started in late June, if I'm not mistaken, because their season starts a lot earlier up there than it does down here. It was typical training camp, meaning it was a lot of hard work.

How long was training camp?

I have no idea. It was more than two weeks. It was probably closer to four weeks before we played our first game up there.

When was your first training camp with the Minnesota Vikings?

That was in 1961, the first year of the Vikings.

Were you drafted by the Vikings or signed as a free agent?

I was traded to the Vikings in the expansion draft. I was playing for the Cleveland Browns at the time.

What was the hardest part about training camp in those days?

The hardest part was learning the various disciplines that you were exposed to. I think the more time you spent in training camp, the better adjusted you became as a player. Especially for me at that time because I was coming in under a whole different system and I needed to understand this coach's system. Our first coach was Norm Van Brocklin, who had an entirely different system than Paul Brown had in Cleveland.

What was the hardest part of practice?

A little bit of everything. The weather was bad in Bemidji. It was cold up there in July, and training camp was long. We had long practices, sometimes as long as two-and-a-half hours, and there was constant running, a lot of hitting. We scrimmaged virtually twice a day.

Can you name some of your teammates back then?

Hugh McElhenny, Fran Tarkenton, of course, Mick Tingelhoff, Jerry Reichow, Bill Bishop, Raymond Hayes, Tom Wilson.

Do you keep in touch with any of the original Vikings today?

Well, throughout the years a lot of the players kept in contact. We do various charitable things together, so we do get to see each other. There were an awful lot of teammates who came and went over the span of my twenty-year career, but I get to see a lot of different people in different parts of the country and it's always fun to meet and catch up with them.

What was your height and weight at the start of your career?

212 pounds, 6 feet 4 inches when I was in Canada. When I came to Cleveland, I was 220. When I came to the Vikings, I stayed around 220-230 pounds for almost my entire career.

Carl Eller's 2004 Hall of Fame ring

Super Bowl XI team photos and press day, 1977

Brent McClanahan and Stu Voigt at the Super Bowl press day, 1977

Vikings fans at the Super Bowl, 1977

Flying to an away game, 1978

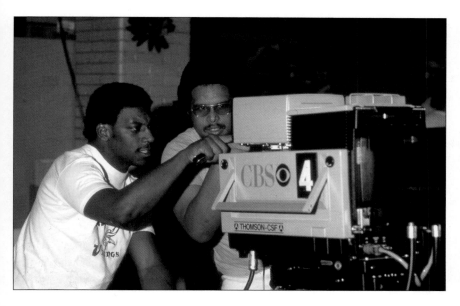

Brent McClanahan and Charles Goodrum play with a CBS camera in the locker room the week of NFC Championship Game, 1976

*Coach Jerry Burns at the Pro Bowl 1979 with Terry Bradshaw (#11)
and Roger Staubach (#12)*

*1976 Vikings linebackers
M. Blair, R. Winston, W. Hilgenberg, Coach J. Nelson, F. McNeil, A. Martin*

*Defense coaches Jocko Nelson, Buddy Ryan and
Neil Armstrong at the Super Bowl XI, 1977*

Fran Tarkenton ABC interview, 1978

Winter at Met Stadium, 1976

Fall at Met Stadium, 1975

Fred Zambreletti makes a formed rib cage for Carl Eller's bruised ribs

Viking's locker room before a practice

Nate Burleson doing push ups as a punishment for dropping a punt

Coach Tice asking defensive player Fred Smoot,
"Would you like to play offense?"

Cris Carter, Matt Blair and Sean
Salisbury on a Vikings' Caribbean cruise

The 2005 defensive team has the potential to play like the '70s' Super Bowl teams

Strength & conditioning coach, Kurtis Schultz, with Brad Johnson during an off season workout

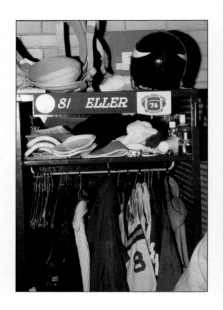

Jim Marshall's locker, 1970s

Carl Eller's locker, 1970s

The locker room at Winter Park

Young fans eagerly get their autographs at training camp, 1977

Fan Village, 2005

Assistant conditioning coach Mark Ellis gives techniques to improve the player's speed

Off season work out at Winter Park

The 2005 offensive line

Muscles need to be stretched and yoga is a part of Viking training

Halftime at the Metrodome, 2004

Randy Moss in the Metrodome, 2003

Alan Page

Bob Berry

Bobby Bryant

Sam McCullum, David Boone,
Autry Beamon, Steve Lawson

Carl Eller

Charles Goodrum and
Brent McClanahan

Nate Wright, Sammy White
and Chuck Foreman

Wally Hilgenberg fooling around in
training camp, 1976

Ahmad Rashad and Robert Miller
pass out fan mail

Kelly Campbell
in training camp, 2005

Vikings fans are the best in the NFL!

How did the name the Purple People Eaters get started?

I think it was one of the newspaper people and an affinity for the song "One eye'd, one horned, flying purple people eaters . . ." or some kind of crazy song like that. They tagged us with that. We never liked it. We thought of ourselves more as the Purple Gang and I think that in Chicago, there was a street gang there called the Purple Gang who were very ruthless. We saw ourselves more of that than the flying Purple People Eaters.

Did you guys have a battle cry in the huddle when you'd come up with the pass rush or stop the running back from running?

If it was a definite passing down, they generally called a coverage call as the line play was called "rush" which meant you had the freedom to do whatever you needed to do to get to the quarterback. And that gave you the freedom to make up games, stunts, between yourself and whoever was playing next to you to get to the quarterback. So other than that, there was no specific thing other than rush.

A lot of players admit to having fallen asleep during the meetings. Did you?

Oh, absolutely. I fell asleep in a lot of the meetings, especially when we had the most boring orders that I've ever heard. He had a monotone voice, and he was always going over things two and three and four times. I'd find me a nice comfortable place on top of the lockers and pull some cover over and go to sleep.

Did you study the film in your playing days to help you improve?

I certainly did. I watched for a lot of stuff. Mostly to pick up different keys you might have as to how a team approached you or how an offensive tackle played against you or different key that a tackle or guard might give you or various formations, and things like that. You learned the best way to overcome what they were trying to do to you. You'd find out if a tackle would line up a little further back if it was a pass, his feet would be more flat and if was going to come out, if it was an aggressive block toward you, he was usually on his toes coming toward you. Things like that.

Did it teach you anything?
I think you learn something everyday. I'm a firm believer that there is something . . . not a day passes that you don't learn something—being able to pay attention to the lesson that's being taught. So of course, I've learned some things over the years.

Did you become friends with any of the players you played against?
Absolutely. I have friends around the league, some who I played against, and of course, some who were at one time or another, my teammates. As I stated before, we get together and associate with each other and help each other in various fundraisers and just kind of replay old times.

Who was the toughest guy you went against?
I'd have to say in my early years, Jim Parker from the Baltimore Colts. He was an All-Pro and of course, a Hall of Fame offensive tackle for the Colts, and he was also my mentor at Ohio State. He kind of brought me up and taught me the game. He was about two years ahead of me and so he kind of took me under his wing and taught me the game. Of course, in my later years, I think the worst game I played was in the Super Bowl against Oakland when Art Shell and Gene Upshaw kept me from making a tackle or a sack the entire game. That was the only time in my career that that ever happened. And it's something that I certainly carry with me everyday.

What was your lowest salary and your highest?
I think my first contract was $18,000 and I think my final contract was about $167,000.

Do you have any comments about the NFL pension?

I think it definitely should improve. I think over the years, we've probably been one of the lowest paid out of the sports, especially if you compare us with baseball. Baseball players retire with certainly a higher retirement than ours. And the various programs they have in baseball, I think, take care of their players. Football, being the type of sport that it is, I think our health plan should be certainly a lot better than it is—along with the retirement benefits.

How is your physical health today?

Not very good. I just had a spinal operation that was not successful. They have to wait for about another six months or so to operate on me again. Hopefully that will get things corrected, but they have to do the same operation over. I have arthritis in my spine. They had to go in and clear up what was interfering with my spinal cord. It's just a result of living the type of life that I lived. I did everything from sky diving to playing football, and that takes its toll on you. I'm also a cancer survivor. I had prostate cancer in 1999 and opted for the new treatment that they had—radioactive seeding into the cancer and that seemed to correct everything. I don't have any indication that I have cancer existing anyplace else in my body.

What was your greatest moment as a player in the NFL?

It was probably the first playoff game that sent us to the Super Bowl, and then the first Super Bowl that we played in back in 1969. It signaled that we accomplished a goal that we had set for ourselves.

How did the slogan 40 for 60 come about?

Joe Kapp came up with that when they chose him for the most valuable player trophy. He said that there was no most valuable Viking—just 40 players for 60 minutes. And that's how that came into being.

You are overdue to be in the Hall of Fame. Why are you not in it yet?

I have no idea. I have nothing to do with it. I've done everything that I can do as a player and it's left up to the people who decide who gets in and who doesn't. If they feel that I'm worthy of being in the Hall of Fame, of course, I'll get in. But if they think that my performance over the twenty-year span that I was in the National Football League isn't worthy of being in the Hall of Fame, then I won't get there.

How many games did you play?

An actual league game, 282, and that's not counting playoff games and Super Bowls and things like that. That is a record in the National Football League, 282 consecutive games. I think there are players that have played more than 282 games, but not consecutively.

And in all those games, what position did you play?

I think Bud put me in every position that there was. He took me out of the game at right tackle and sent me in at guard. Then he sent me in at tight end. I guess this was his way of allowing me to line up in every position that I played. Still, I had to ask whoever I was playing next to what I was supposed to do in that position.

Could you list four important things that you would talk to kids about on sports and education?

Look at life as a learning experience. I think that if you make it fun—because I think learning has to be fun, and to me it was always a game, you know, what can I learn today that's going to make me a little bit better? What can I learn today that's going to help me a little more? Those are the kinds of things that, when I go out to talk to kids, I encourage them to do, to look at learning as something that is not restricting, but as a freedom that we have. It's something that will free you for the rest of your life. It gives you more options. I always encourage kids to always learn as much as they can about as many things as they can because one time or another in life, it's going to be valuable. I think parents have an obligation to guide their young people. You can't dictate to them, but you certainly can guide them in a very positive direction. Help them to learn as much as they can possibly learn. Teach them the disciplines that we need to have as a functioning human being. If you kind of follow these guidelines, I think you can raise a good crop of young people.

What message do you have for the Minnesota Vikings football fans that have cheered you on over the years?

I'd certainly thank them. I meet people on a daily basis who tell me how much they enjoyed watching me play. They certainly don't know their cheering out there was a far greater experience to me. I really felt that I was doing something that was significant and brought a lot of happiness and joy to an awful lot of people and that is something that I will always carry with me. Hopefully, they'll always feel about the Minnesota Vikings the way I feel about them.

How does it feel to be fortunate enough to play in four Super Bowls?

We were very proud, of course, to have the opportunity to play in four Super Bowls. There are a lot of players in the National Football League and players in the Hall of Fame in these later years who didn't play in one Super Bowl, so we feel very fortunate playing in four. It's a disappointment that I will always carry with me that we never won and we had four chances to win and didn't win any of those games.

How did the defense manage to play so great at times and to win as much as they did?

I think it was because we played together for so long that we had an understanding of our strengths and weaknesses. We knew how to compensate in various situations for some of the adversities that we had. I think all of us enjoyed playing football together and in the end, we had one common goal—and that was to win.

Knowing what you know now, is there anything that you would do differently then on or off the field?

I don't know. There are so many things that knowing what I know now, I would approach them a little differently, but I think it's like that with everything that we do in life. Like I said, it's a constant learning experience. Overall, I've had a wonderful life. I've enjoyed myself and plan to continue to enjoy myself. Hopefully someone will see something positive out of my life experience and it will help them to see how they can take their life experience in the positive direction I have taken mine.

#81   CARL ELLER

DEFENSIVE LINE   1964-1978

Photo taken 1976

STATS

HIGH SCHOOL
Name of School: Atkins High School
Location of School: Winston-Salem, North
    Carolina
Graduation year: 1960
Position: Offensive, Defensive Tackle
Jersey number: 65
Height: 6 feet 4 inches
Weight: 220 pounds
Coach: Coach Ben Warren
Other sports played: Track and field

COLLEGE
Name of School: University of Minnesota
Location of School: Minneapolis, Minnesota
How long attended: 3 1/2 years
Did you graduate? Yes, Metropolitan State
    University (BA degree)
Degree: MA & PhD, Sacramento Regent
    University
Position: Offensive Tackle, Defensive Tackle
Jersey number: 76
Height: 6 feet 6 inches
Weight: 245 pounds
40 speed: 4.6 seconds
Coach: Murray Warmath
Other sports played: None

PRO
Position: Defensive End
Jersey number: 81
Year Drafted: 1964
Draft Round: First
Year Retired: 1980
Height: 6 feet 6 inches
Weight: 255 pounds
40 speed: 4.5 seconds
Coaches: Norm Van Brocklin, Bud Grant

How did it feel when you were drafted to be a Viking right from the University of Minnesota?

It was great to be a Minnesota Viking and be drafted right from the University of Minnesota. I really like this area and I wanted to stay. Back then the Vikings were a young team and it was great to be part of that.

Do you remember what time of day it was when they called you?

I think it was in the midday. It was midday because they had an early draft. There were some other teams that expressed a little interest, so I wasn't sure I'd make it to the Vikes.

Who called you to tell you that you made the team?

I think it was their coach. It wasn't John Michaels, he came later, but Montgomery, he was one of Norm Van Brocklin's assistant coaches, like the backfield coach.

Who else was drafted out of Minnesota that year?

Milt Sundae was drafted that year. Milt Sundae was drafted twentieth round by the Vikings. We were in the same class and the same year, so we joined the Vikings the same year. Milt played starting guard for a number of years. He must have played eight or nine years in the league.

Is there a time in your college career when you knew you were going to go pro?

I think that by my junior year I knew the pros were interested because I started to get letters—they sent them to almost everybody they were interested in. I was All-American Second Team in my junior year, so I felt like I had a good chance.

Did your team go to any of the Rose Bowls?

Yes, they did. In fact, I went to the Rose Bowl my sophomore year, and we beat UCLA. My team actually had gone the year before my freshman year, but we weren't eligible.

How hard was it for you to make the Vikings team? Was there any competition when they drafted you number one?

I was drafted number one so I knew that they were going to make a spot for me on the roster, but I wasn't really sure how well I'd do. I did know they had the defensive end position for me, so I felt like all I had to do was prove myself.

Did you start your rookie year?

Yes, I started my rookie year and I started the first game, but I didn't start in pre-season because I was away at All-Star camp.

What professional team did your All-Stars play?

We played the Bears, I think.

So they had won the title that year.

The '63 Bears, yeah.

This was before the Super Bowl. What was it called then?

It was the NFL Championship game. That was equal to the Super Bowl because it was all just one team left at the top.

What did you think about training camp?

In training camp, you'd always have to go back and test yourself and make sure you're in shape to get out on the field and get going and really get into it, you know . . . that really was fun. The first few days were always pretty exciting, but then after that, it was kind of more or less the dorm after curfew.

Did you miss curfew at all during any of the training camps?

I might have missed one or two but not many. It's like getting back from downtown or something, trying to beat the clock. You know, those kinds of things.

Who was your roommate your first year?

Jim Marshall was my roommate the whole time—maybe fifteen, sixteen years—on the road, as well.

How were the relationships between the rookies and the veterans?

That was something that was different about the Vikings. They really did try to bring their younger players along and try to help them out, particularly if they had some good quality in them and some talent.

The way you answered that is like you want the rookies to make the team so they can be on the special teams so you wouldn't have to!

That's a good thought.

During the regular season, what was your schedule during the week?

Typically, in those days, you didn't have the variety of game days. Pretty much you played on Sunday and every once in a while, you'd play a Saturday or a Monday night. Typically, on a Monday, you'd go in and watch films and loosen up and get in the hot tub or whatever and then Tuesdays were normally a day off. Monday was typically an early day so you'd go in and be done by noon, but during the week, with [Norm] Van Brocklin, it varied. Some days you'd meet maybe four to five hours and other days it would only be an hour. It would depend on what his mood was.

So compared to the guys today it seems like it's 24-7.

Well, yeah, it does. I have no idea what they do today. It can't be that much to study. But I know there is more conditioning today and things like that. I think once you get it down, you need to relax and have something other than football on your mind for a while.

What is one of your rookie mistakes that you made?
One of my rookie mistakes was going in to tackle Johnny Unitas. He was a hero of mine and I was getting ready to sack him, you know. I had him dead in my sights and he threw the ball under-arm and completed a pass. I learned from that.

How did it feel to be in the Super Bowl?
It was great to be in the Super Bowl. That was one of our better years and better teams, and I felt like we were going to be World Champions. I felt like we had the team to go in there and beat the Chiefs, but they were very tough opponents. They were tougher than maybe we gave them credit for. They had a lot more weapons, you know, like Jan Stenerud. Man, he could kick that ball from the middle of the field and score every time.

The Purple People Eaters. When did it start and what year do you think was your best year as a defensive team?
I think the Purple People Eaters started around the first Super Bowl. I can't remember if it started before that. Our best team was probably in those years between the years of the Chiefs and the Dolphins game—'69, '70, '71.

Who was the hardest running back to bring down in your time?
That was a tough one because I always had a great respect for Gayle Sayers. He was just such a dangerous back. He could score from anywhere, you know, more than anybody I've ever seen. He's just one of a lot of them. I think [Walter] Payton, Jim Brown, who I didn't play that much, Franco Harris, you know, they were all really tough.

Who is the toughest quarterback to bring down?

Roger Staubach was tough to get to and to bring down. [Roman] Gabriel was hard to bring down. [Joe] Namath was tough to get to because of his quick release, and [Johnny] Unitas had a great respect for his field.

You broke your hand and had it in a cast, and you still played. Tell us something about that.

I broke it on a fluke play. The running back came out and did a kind of a wheel kick, and I tried to protect myself and his heel came up and hit my hand. I was pretty much injury free most of my career. I had one knee injury, but I hadn't really missed any games. So I got my hand fixed and put a cast on it to protect it and I kept on playing, but it was just one of those things. It wasn't really a major injury—just broken in an area where they needed to put a pin in it.

Most players played with pain back in the day, but you didn't work out. Were you guys just tougher?

Well, it wasn't that we didn't work out, we did work out. We did really strenuous work outs and really hard practices on the field. We were really well conditioned in terms of the cardiovascular, but we didn't do as much with weights, though. Most guys did something to condition themselves by either running or doing some kind of calisthenics or something like that.

How many sacks have you had?

My stats are 134 1/2 sacks is what I think stands as my record, but they didn't start to really keep sacks records until after I left the game. In the early '80s is when they started to keep them, and I retired in '80. I probably had 20-30 more sacks than they gave me credit for. But the other thing too is that I played the runs really well. That was a big part and most of the time it was maybe 40-60 run the pass or 40-60 run the pass run, so stopping the runner was really important too, it wasn't just all sacking the quarterback. That's something that just kind of came along after I played. You had to be able to do both, you know? I took a great deal of pride in being able to stop the run too.

What part of the game today—compared to when you played—is harder?

Well, I think for most guys, it's harder to rush the passer because they can grab you and hold you, which was illegal. Of course, they'd get penalized for that. They're also a lot larger so you're not going to get the push on these guys. You have to be a much bigger defensive guy to match up with them strengthwise.

Are the referees better or worse, or do they need to go to school to get better?

I don't really know. It's hard to comment because you need to be on the field to tell if the refs are doing a good job.

You were recently inducted into the NFL Hall of Fame. How many have entered the Hall of Fame?

There are 225 people all total and about 190 of those are actual players.

How did you feel when they told you that you were inducted into the Hall of Fame?

Well, it was a great feeling. It was something that encapsulates your career. It puts a stamp on your career and it speaks for you. It's a great thing and a great honor because all the guys in there that really played well and accomplished a lot are the players who I admired too. It's great company, so I really liked that part.

What advice would you give the young players coming up in high school or junior high?

Well, I've started The Carl Eller Foundation. Basically, we are working with young kids, all males, mostly African American males. We are trying to get them to be leaders and, to do that, we want to give them the tools to be leaders and help them knock down the barriers so they are able to get through high school and into college and on.

Give three things that kids should do to be a better student in school.
One thing would be to develop a passion for reading. That's going to be your best tool. Two is to listen to your teacher and really try to learn in math or writing—those are really big skills. But everyone doesn't have an acumen for it, so you really have to try and work and develop those skills. Number three would be to really get exposed to as many opportunities as you can. Don't be close-minded, don't say no to things that you don't know about. Take that opportunity to explore and to learn.

What is your favorite food?
I think my favorite meal is a steak. I like to grill a steak. It's very simple: grilled steak and potato. That's it—with a nice loaf of bread or something.

Those guys you played with on the line, the Purple People Eaters, who were they and what do they mean to you off the field?
Gary Larson, Jim Marshall, and Alan Page. I mean playing with those guys was great; they were like brothers. We were like brothers on the field, and they are like brothers off the field. It's a camaraderie that still exists today. It's just a great love for those guys and a great respect. They were fun to play with, they gave their all, they were there to stand by you, and it's a real, real privilege to have played with those guys.

When you were in the huddle, what would you say?
"We'll meet at the quarterback!"

After the interview, as Matt and Carl sat and chatted, Matt shared this fond memory with Carl:
It was a pre-game meal before the Houston–Viking home game back in about '76 and we were at the Registry Hotel. We walked in for our pre-game meal which has always been a standard baked

potato, steak, and the normal honey, butter, etc. Keep in mind that this is in the morning hours, prior to a noon game.

Well, Carl walks in and, in front of all the coaches and players, he demands pancakes. Coach Grant doesn't even look up and continues to eat his meal; typical Bud Grant, no comment or eye contact.

The room grows quiet as Carl sits down and then he shouts again, "I want pancakes!" and then the serving trays, dishes, everything goes flying. And the last thing we see is Carl marching out the door shouting, "I want pancakes!"

Bud still doesn't look up, he continues eating and we, as young players didn't know what to expect next. So we went to the game, and we play Houston, and we thought as young players we better play our butts off after what just happened, and we beat the Oilers 55-7.

At our Monday morning team meeting, Mr. Eller apologized to the group, coaches, and everyone present. The following pre-game meal, we have our standard potatoes, eggs, steaks, and whatever, and right in front of Carl, they served some silver dollar pancakes on the side. That was a one-time change in our menu for that game only.

#75 BOB LURTSEMA

TACKLE

1972-1976

Photo taken 2005

HIGH SCHOOL

Name of School: Ottawa Hills High Sch[
Location of School: Grand Rapids, Mic[
Graduation Year: 1960
Position: Offensive Tackle, Defensive T[
Number: 15
Height: 6 feet 6 inches
Weight: 185 pounds
Coach: Rip Collins
Other sports played: Basketball and Ba[

COLLEGE

Name of School: Grand Rapids Junior College,
    Michigan Tech, Western Michigan
Location of School: Grand Rapids; Houghton,
    Michigan; and Kalamazoo, Michigan
Graduation Year: 1962, 1967
How long attended: two years, one year, 2 1/2 years
Did you graduate? Yes, No, Yes
Degree: Mechanics engineering
Position: Defensive Tackle, Defensive Tackle,
    and Tight End
Number: 91, 96, 89
Height: 6 feet 6 inches
Weight: 195, 210, 240 pounds
40 speed: 4.85 seconds
Coach: Gordy Hunsburger, Omer LaJeunesse,
    Billy Doolittle
Other sports played: Basketball and baseball

PRO

Position: Defensive Tackle
Number: Colts, #78; Giants, #71;
    Vikings #75; Seahawks #70
Free Agent/Other: Free Agent 1966
Year Retired: 1978
Height: 6 feet 6 inches
Weight: 255 pounds
40 speed: 4.85 seconds
Coaches: Don Shula, Allie Sherman,
    Alex Webster, Bud Grant, Jack
    Pattera

Who did you play for before becoming a Viking?

I was with the New York Giants for five years. They were so bad. I was a starter and a player rep with them in the '71 season. I did a survey for the owner, Mr. Mara, because he felt he was losing rapport with the team. I talked to everybody on the team and nobody liked him. I told Mr. Mara the truth and that was at 1:30 on a Tuesday and I was on waivers at 4:30 on the same day. I'd say I lost some steps—I played seven more years a half a step slower. After that I came to the Viking's in the 11th game of '71.

In the '71 season, you had a chance to play with some of the greatest defensive players aligned in the NFL. What did you bring to them?

I brought motivation. [Carl] Eller, [Jim] Marshall and [Alan] Page always felt I'd beat them out of their position, and they'd be embarrassed, so I was the driving force to keep them going! But we came together from a confidence standpoint. Being a regular for those five years, it wasn't like I was coming in like a rookie or anything. They embraced me and my attitude because of the ups and downs that we did, and the first day I was there, Coach Patera worked me a little harder than normal.

Do you feel you were picked on?

Oh, yeah! I'm doing ups and downs and they would throw the ball so long, I didn't have any legs left. So I fell flat on my face. Then I got up and fell flat on my face again. Bud saw that, turned his head and walked away. I figured that was my last day as a Viking, but I also think that's when the players kind of picked up and said, "Hey, Lurtsema's got heart."

How tough was training camp for you?

I loved training camp. I really did. A lot pf people came down and they complained and were negative—they don't like this, they don't like that. We came down, we worked hard, and I came in the best of shape because I had to make it with effort and attitude. I knew that, and it wasn't a problem. Just being around the players, playing cards, going down to Shakey's Pizza, we'd run down there for three minutes to grab our pop or whatever else we wanted and hustled back because we had to be back by six. I liked camp because psychologically you'll pass out before you'll die. I've always felt that. It didn't bother me.

Of your time being a Viking, which season do think was the best?

1972. We didn't even make the playoffs. We were 7-7 that year, but the defensive line was all in their prime. We were the number-one defense in the league, but we had a couple bad breaks. We'd lose some games that weren't really even high scoring games, but the group itself, that's when they were at their peak. After that they started to tail down a little bit—not much, but a little bit.

Why is Bob Lurtsema's name in Minnesota bigger than guys like Alan Page who was the league MVP?

That's a good question! It probably had to do with the three hundred commercials I did with TCF. They called me Benchwarmer Bob because I was backing up the front four. I think the reason people still remember me is that I'm a goofball in the commercials, but, when you meet me in person, I'm the same way—I'm the same person who's been in their home for over thirteen years.

What has football done for you and your family?

Everything. I had passion for the game, and I have Benchwarmer Bob's Sports Café, of course, and I have the Viking Update newspaper. I owe everything to football. I knew that from day one. I always felt it was an honor to play in the National Football League—not a right. I owe everything to football.

Other than Benchwarmer Bob's Café, how did you invest your money?

In the '70's, John Beasley and a few of us bought a silver mine called the Golden Chest Mine. John Beasley had a relative and he had the mineral rights out in Murray, Idaho. So, believe it or not, ten days ago, Jim Marshall, Bob Barry, John Beasley, and Bob Lurtsema, we flew back there. Thirty-one years ago, that same group went out to those mines and the NFL films did a special on us. So here we are thirty years later, old timers right down to Jim and his cane because he just had an operation on his back, going back to see where their gold is. That was one of the investments I got into, and I lucked out that way. When I retired from football though, I continued to work sixty hours a week. But it really isn't work. I love what I do, but you got to pay the fiddler—and I must say I paid the fiddler.

Is there really gold out there?

Yeah, there is. It's a new mine. Gold is up $15.00 the last three days. They might have a $100 million vein in there. It's for real. The special will be on in November.

Do you have any teammates that you still keep in touch with over the years?

I have a tremendous amount of friends. Mick Tingelhoff comes down here to camp all the time. We had a real core of people, because Paul Krause developed some land and Ahmad Rashad bought from there. Dave Osborn bought from there, Tingelhoff lives out in the area. Tommy Kramer rented, but I wish he would have bought. I see Jim Marshall all the time. Jim and I are the best of friends and Moose [Carl Eller] of course, when he and I get talking, we automatically begin laughing about our fun times throughout our NFL careers. So there's a good fifteen to twenty people I see all the time who are good friends.

What were your lowest and highest contract amounts?

My lowest was $9,000. That was '66. I thought I robbed and stole from the poor. And then my last year, my twelfth year in the league, I had a base of $55,000 with a lock of $15,000 clause in there if I was playing half a season. I made $70,000 at the peak and that was 1977.

Did you make more money doing commercials than you did playing football?

Oh yeah! Hey, Mike Lynn nailed me one time. Mike got me two years in a row for $40,000 because I did not want to negotiate with the guy. Then I really got back at Mike. What goes around, comes around. I saw Mike at a function and I went up to him and said, "I want to tell you something. I'm speaking from the heart, Mr. Lynn. I would have signed for less." He knows I would have and that just got his goat so much. I would have signed for less for one main reason—I love the Twin Cities area. When you come from

New York with the traffic and the crime there, and then you come to Minneapolis, you have the theater, you have the arts, and you have professional football, basketball, baseball, soccer, you have everything. You're ten minutes away from everything.

What can you say about Jim Marshall?

That's the greatest man in the world. He was our team captain and you'd follow him anywhere. I mean, his endurance factor and the level he brought. You had to stay up to his level because they would call you out. That, to me, is the part about both ends. Carl Eller and Jim Marshall, they'd call you out if you didn't play. I liked that because when you're not doing your job, there's nothing like a little kick in the fanny to wake you up. That's what made it so unique. But I can't say enough good things about that man.

What about Gary Larson?

Gary Larson was kind of . . . they always said, "Three dots and a dash." They kind of kidded themselves about that. He was the only white lineman, of course. He was kind of the catalyst that brought everyone . . . if you talk about racial issues, and I don't like to, and I don't care what color anybody is, but that was the bond. In other words, they knew that he was running with that group up there and everyone was running with him. Because he's good people and they're good people. So Larson, as good as the team was, he had another intangible to bring everybody together.

What about Carl Eller?

I said earlier that when I came to the Vikings, all I had was conditioning, heart, and attitude. Carl never lifted a weight, he
never did a thing. The first day of camp he made me look like a
fool! He was in good shape and stronger and all that, but he
had the God-given talents and physical attributes to just be a
natural at what he was. And his sense of humor and his laugh
plus his total dominance of the offensive line was something
special.

And the last guy on the front four, Alan Page?

During his playing years, he pulled some tricks on me. One time
he left an iron lung in the basement of my new house. Where he
got it from, I don't know, but I came home one dark evening and
there it was. But it was fun playing with Alan because he was so
good. He was the defensive player of the year averaging 12-13
tackles per game and it should be 3-5. He was so quick getting off
the ball. The front four would play the stunt game when I came in
as the fifth defensive lineman on pass rush and run stunts and, if I
said something and wanted to do something, he'd say "great"
because there would be a chance that it might work and vice versa.
Alan always said that education always comes first. That's the
speech he gives to everybody even in his induction speech for the
Hall of Fame. And that's why he's a Supreme Court Judge right
now. That's the way you want to progress. But what a football
player!

How would you advise kids about education and sports?

As far as a kid's education goes, in life, every day is a learning
experience. If you are the last person on the ladder of success,
if you're on the first step and can't get out of that but you're
trying as hard as you can, don't ever be embarrassed about

your effort because you've earned the respect of other people around you. Once you know from inside that you've given the best that you can, you're going to be respected by the other people around you. If you're working hard, then they can't make fun of you. You can not advance unless you get as much education as you can. But I think that if you take the attitude that you're going to do the best that you can, then everything will really fall in place rather easily and you can become very, very successful.

#54   FRED MCNEILL

LINEBACKER   1974-1985

Photo taken 2005

STATS

HIGH SCHOOL
Name of School: Baldwin Park High Sch◦
Location of School: Baldwin Park, Califo◦
Graduation Year: 1970
Position: Running Back and Linebacker
Height: 6 feet 2 inches
Weight: 205 pounds
Other sports played: Basketball and trac◦
    ran high and low hurdles, 400-yard, r◦
    relay

COLLEGE
Name of School: UCLA
Location of School: West Los Angeles,
    California
Graduation Year: 1977
How long attended: 1970 to 1977
Did you graduate? Yes
Degree: Economics
Position: Defensive End in a 5-2 defense
Number: 92
Height: 6 feet 2 inches
Weight: 225 pounds
40 speed: 4.45 seconds
Coach: Pepper Rodgers
Other sports played: Ran hurdles part time
    because of conflict with football

PRO
Position: Linebacker
Number: 54
Year Drafted: 1974
Draft Round: First
Year Retired: 1985
Height: 6 feet 2 inches
Weight: 230 pounds
40 speed: 4.4 seconds
Coach : Bud Grant 1974 to approxi-
    mately 1983, then Less Steckle
    1984, and then Bud Grant again in
    1985.

In your rookie year, did you find training camp hard?

Probably the hardest thing for me in terms of rookie camp was the psychological part, the fear of getting cut. Mainly because at that point you expect that you are going to run a lot—and we did. We had two-a-days and we had meetings in between and we had meetings at night. You had to eat a lot of food at lunch or they'd think you're a wimp. But in terms of how difficult it was, probably the most difficult part was the psychological part of wondering if you'd make the team. And if you're going to get a chance to play or they'll realize they made a mistake drafting you.

Did anything funny happen during training camp?

As rookies, you had to stand up on a chair and sing. They had to sing the National Anthem or their school fight song from college. With me it was the Bruins, and we had such an easy fight song, but if I remember correctly, it was just mediocre. I did just mediocre. And actually, that was the beginning of my singing career!

What were the hardest things for you in training camp?

The part I didn't like in terms of practice was probably when we started doing our conditioning. I don't remember if it was my rookie year or when it was, when they told over thirty guys to go in and they had the rookies run, and we worked out while the old guys went in and took a break. The majority of the players back then were over thirty.

Did anything happen on the rookie floor that you can tell us about? Did you get in trouble?

You know, it's interesting that one evening, I won't say who it was, but I walked in on one of the players who was having a really good

---

FRED MCNEILL

time in one of the rooms with one of the cheerleaders from the cities in Mankato. But I won't say who it was even though his name begins with a . . . I won't mention who he was.

What happened before the College All-Star game that you and I were playing in?

I do remember that someone suggested to me that to relax in the game, I should take muscle relaxers. Which I never did, but I can't remember who suggested that, but you and I were roommates there too. I remember that at one point I was going to go get some chips or something from the store and I asked you if you wanted some chips. It was kind of coincidental that you and I would get drafted by the same team and be roommates while we were at the All-Star game and after rookie year.

Matt: So what actually happened?

Fred: What actually happened? Well, I don't remember.

Matt: Fred, don't you remember the All-Star game was cancelled?

Fred: It was?

Matt: Fred, Fred, Fred. This is when the college All-Star team played the NFL Super Bowl team in 1974. What happened?

Fred: Wait a minute . . . are you talking . . .

Matt: Fred, when the college All-Stars played the Miami Dolphins, don't you remember that? We were picketed by Alan Page and some of the other players in the NFL who came down to Chicago and picketed and didn't want us to have the game because they were on strike. So Frank Gilliam told us to get our butts back to Minnesota because they had cancelled the All-Star game. It was in Chicago and so he got us on a plane and got us both out of there and we went on to camp.

And of course, camp . . . do you remember anything about the strike?

Fred: Well I do remember something about the strike, but remind me more about this All-Star game you were talking about because I guess I should remember.

Matt: It was the last one ever played. Well, we didn't get to play in it. But that was the last one that was supposed to be played—they cancelled it. They didn't have anymore after that. Let's go back to the strike year. Do you remember anything about it?

Fred: I remember that we were in the place of a position, as rookies, in a position of whether we were going to cross over the picket line. I don't really remember players standing out picketing. But we were placed in a position of making a difficult choice—whether or not we were going to cross the line or not.

Matt: My memory is that we crossed the line, we went to camp, because we were rookies. As a matter of fact, we played as rookies. Our first game that we played as rookies, we were in Denver and the middle linebacker we had who was drafted—he couldn't remember all the plays, he couldn't remember all the signals. Luckily I was able to remember some of the signals and Coach asked me to make the calls for us. We then went out to Denver and played and it was a good experience for us because there were no veterans in the game at all or in camp. We played and came back and we lost the game, but we played. So anyway, back to the interview.

Later on in your career you were a player representative. Is that right?
Yes, that's true.

What did being a player representative entail?
As a player representative, my responsibility was to relay information to the players. It was to understand the position the players

had and the issues they had. When we'd go back to the players' rep meeting that the NFL Players Association (NFLPA) would have, our job was to convey information to the NFLPA group and also to take information from those meetings back to the players.

Was being a players' rep hard because, through you, the management would think that the players could strike against the owners, so the owners would get rid of most of the players' reps?

At that point, we had heard stories about players who weren't playing because they were blackballed for being players' reps, or that they had advocated or supported the NFL Players Association. So that was something that was always on our mind. But I remember—I think it was that year that we played in the Hall of Fame Game—the players had decided they wanted to display their unity out on the field, and as they lined up before the game to sing the National Anthem, the NFLPA representatives had all agreed that we were going to have the players from each side of the team walk across and meet in mid-field and shake hands. I really had a difficult time conveying to Bud Grant that we were going to take that stand at the game and walk across and meet the other team at mid-field and shake their hands showing our unity as a union of players. That was unusual because you only have a limited time before a game, and when the players walked across and shook hands, that threw a lot of things off for the TV broadcasts and in the set structure of the NFL games and how they start. But, in the end, we were recognized as a unified group playing against each other.

You were drafted in the first round. What was it like back then?

Some of my teammates were surprised that I was paid so much. I had a $100,000 signing bonus. The money was certainly different compared to today.

During the draft, were the press around like they are today?

No. They were there for Fran [Tarkenton] and other stars, but not so much for linebackers like me. To tell you the truth, I was at my apartment and my brother Rod was with me. I had heard prior to the draft that I was going to get drafted by a team in the NFL. It wasn't the Vikings; it was San Diego or something. We were just sitting around the apartment waiting to find out. As a matter of fact, I was actually surprised that I would get drafted, but the only thing that I recall happened was that I got a call from my agent saying that I was going to get drafted by Tommy Prothro down with the San Diego Chargers. At that time there was the World Football League and I was told that I was going to get drafted if I agreed to accept a certain amount and didn't do any negotiations. Then later I got a phone call that I was being drafted by the Vikings in the first round, seventeenth pick.

What do you recall about when you were a rookie and the team practiced at the St. Paul Stadium?

The stadium didn't have very much to offer, but that was our practice facility. If anything was good about it, it was the fact that it was in St. Paul and we had a lot of space that we could use without a lot of people bothering us. We didn't have any weights or any other sort of practice facility there, but we had weights over at Met Stadium. Still, it wasn't very big. The only thing we had was a very small room.

At the Met on Saturday Mornings, you were on "The donut patrol." You had to bring so many donuts on Saturday mornings, and if you didn't bring them, what would Bud do?

He'd make us run those stadium steps if we didn't bring donuts. But I also remember that we used to bring those donuts and then after awhile, we decided donuts weren't that healthy. And then we started bringing fruit.

How did you feel when you made the Vikings team knowing only five linebackers made the team the year before?

I was happy to make the team, but the competition to make the team and to be a contributing player continued. I continued with this necessity to make the playing squad, and to make plays and to contribute to a win. Further, to be a leader on the team was part of the driving force.

How did that feel to play in the 1974 Super Bowl in your rookie year?

Well, obviously this was an exciting game for us. I remember you blocking an extra point and [Bill] Brown recovered it for our only score. Then we missed an extra point and it was 16-6 and we lost to the Steelers that game. In Super Bowl XI, I blocked a punt and Wally [Hilgenberg] recovered it but we didn't score. Brent McClanahan fumbled on the two-yard line. Unfortunately, he still has people who give him trouble about that even today. One time, we were at a place signing autographs and someone came up to him and said, "I can't believe you fumbled the ball." I turned to Brent and asked him, "Man, do you always hear stuff like that?" and he said, "Yeah, people are always coming up to me and talking about how I fumbled the ball." He still feels bad about it.

Thirty years later, does it still haunt you for having not won a Super Bowl after playing in two of them?

I was very disappointed because, recently, the Vikings were in contention for getting to the Super Bowl and I was hoping they were going to win. But in general, in terms of people who you meet, I have a Super Bowl ring and, when you meet people, they look at it and say "Wow! Nice ring!" and I always say, "But we didn't win." But generally, what people remember is that you got there. They appreciate the fact that the team was successful enough to get to the Super Bowl—four Super Bowls. But I guess that it's always in my mind that they know that we didn't win.

Do you think that with a victory in the Super Bowl, the Viking organization will not be haunted anymore?

It's something that really haunts teams even though you got there. We do need to win one to get rid of this stigma or whatever to get this monkey off our back. Especially when we walk in a room and there's Oakland Raiders' Rod Martin in the room with two to three Super Bowl Championship rings. Rod's a great guy, but he always has to mention the fact that I have a Super Bowl ring that's not the winner's ring. All the guys who won Super Bowls, they talk loudly and boldly about winning a Super Bowl. And it hurts that you've been there twice and didn't win. I'd like to see the Vikings win so that I can say that they've won at least one in our lifetime.

What was special about going to games out of town where you had family? How many tickets did you need?

I always needed a lot if it was where my family was going to be. This was especially true when we played in the 1977 Super Bowl Game versus the Raiders. When we were in California, all my immediate family was there as well as other family I had on the east coast. I was able to get tickets for family and friends who could come to the game. As a matter of fact, now I run into friends and they still say, "Yeah, thanks Fred, for giving me the tickets back in '76-'77 Super Bowl." It was nice we were able to get tickets, and I always enjoyed getting together with my family after the game.

What would you want to tell the Vikings fans who supported you all the years of playing in Minnesota?

I've learned that the Vikings fans are very loyal and very supportive. When you walk into a stadium and walk out onto the field for a game, it really does matter. When you hear your fans cheering you on to win, it really does make a big difference in the game and how you're able to fight to the end. It still goes on even today when I meet the Southern California Vikings Fan Club and go to different cities and meet people, who are avid fans. It's just really great to play for a team that has a true tradition and a tradition that people really love and support over a period of time for a long time. I appreciate it and having played for the Minnesota Vikings was a great part of my life.

What advice do you have for kids pertaining to education and sports?

All the kids need to know that playing sports is a wonderful experience. You can compete in sports and compete in education as well. One of the things that you can tell if you look at my experience in life is that you can have fun and enjoy life, and that is more than sports. So go ahead and compete in sports and have a good time and learn all the fundamentals and all the things that are important to your success, but understand that there is more in life than just sports.

#59   MATT BLAIR

LINEBACKER   1974-1985

Photo taken 2001

S T A T S

HIGH SCHOOL
Name of School: Colonel White High
    School
Location of School: Dayton, Ohio
Graduation Year: 1969
Position: Wide Receiver and Safety
Jersey number: 82
Height: 6 feet 2 1/2 inches
Weight: 180 pounds
40 speed: 4.9 seconds
Coach: Jim Elby
Other sports played: Football, basketball,
    baseball, track

COLLEGE
Name of Schools: Northeastern A & M and Iowa State
    University
Location of Schools: Miami, Oklahoma, and Ames,
    Iowa, respectively
Graduation Year: 1974
How long attended: 4 1/2 years (red shirt)
Did you graduate? Yes
Degree: Physical Education, minor in Driver's
    Education
Position: Defensive Back at NEO, Strong Safety at ISU
Jersey number: 90 at NEO, 47 at ISU
Height: 6 feet 5 1/2 inches
Weight: 225 pounds
40 speed: 4.75 seconds
Coach: Chuck Bowman at NEO, Johnny Majors at ISU
Other sports played: Basketball

PRO
Position: Strong Outside
    Linebacker, Middle
    Linebacker on passing
    game
Jersey number: 59
Year Drafted: 1974
Draft Round: Second
Year Retired: 1986
Height: 6 feet 5 1/2 inches
Weight: 240 pounds
40 speed: 4.65 seconds
Coach: Bud Grant, Les Steckel

What was the process for you to become a Viking?

After I made the junior college team, I told my parents they only had a half-year scholarship and it wouldn't pay for the full ride. I had to ask that if the opportunity would present itself, would they be able to help me out financially. My dad had retired from the Air Force and was working at the State of Ohio Correctional Facility in Dayton and my mom didn't work. They said, "Stay there, we'll send you money. You stay in school and get your education." I didn't know it at the time, but I later learned that my parents had given up two or three months rent to keep me in school. Because they put themselves in debt, I was able to stay in school.

Despite my best efforts at the junior college, I didn't have the right grades to get into school, so I had to work harder. I attended First Baptist Church. At the church, I met some great people and had the opportunity to get to know them and they helped me along the way. Joe and Dortha Gorley helped me tremendously. They are like my second parents. And then Mrs. Price helped me with my education. She helped me with my studies and everything else so I could get the passing grades that I needed. It certainly didn't hurt that her husband was the team doctor. So it all worked well.

That year, 1969, we went undefeated, but I never made the team's starting roster. I was a backup. I wasn't even on the traveling squad. I wanted to do more, so I continued to work harder. To be an athlete, you have to put the time into it.

After achieving a point—both mentally and physically—I made the traveling squad, and we went undefeated that year which took us to Savannah, Georgia, and we won the Junior College National Championship. I had a taste of football. I knew how far I had gone, and what I could do. To keep myself at the top of my physical game, I went out for the basketball team. It quickly became my second-favorite sport. On the basketball team, I was looked at as a bit of a brute. I was seen as a big football player pushing around basketball players on the court and I loved that, not to mention that the coach used me a lot because of that. I was playing the sixth man, coming off the bench and as a starter at times. I didn't average very much, but I was a good rebounder.

I became good at what I was doing. It was just one of those things that you look at your life and you think back about how much better I'd have been at things, if I worked harder. In basketball, we were seventh in the nation and we went to the finals and got beat by a guy named Rob Macadoo, and they went on to win. They were from Mobile, Indiana, and went on to win the championship.

I physically grew that summer after my freshman year in college. No, I didn't take any supplements and, no, I didn't take any steroids, but I grew three inches and gained about 45 pounds in three months. I came back to NEO and the coaches just took one look at me and said, "Where would you like to play?" Of course I wanted to play, so they put me in at a stand-up linebacker, strong safety, and defensive back. I was able to play all three positions. We lost one game and, after that, I was in a position to move on. I was recruited from all over—for basketball as well.

In the end, I decided that I wanted to play football. I was bigger at my position than most guys were and I decided that basketball wasn't the sport for me. Besides, there are too many seven-footers out there playing guard and I didn't want to be a shrimp among them.

Iowa State had recruited me, but because I got there in the spring, I already knew that I'd be a non-starter. At least I was accustomed to it. They put me on the fourth team, in a black jersey. I knew it was time to work. The harder I worked each week, I got another color jersey and moved up to yellow, then red. And, of course, the last week in spring ball, to a white jersey which was the first team. That fall, in '71, I started with the Cyclones at Iowa State. Coaches were Johnny Majors (head coach) and my personal coach at monster back (which is a weak side, strong safety) was Jackie Sherrill, and I was a starter at that position and excelled the best I could. That year we were 8-3 and, for the first time in the ISU's history, we went to a Bowl game.

From that point, the confidence in me had grown. I had grown as a player. The responsibilities of knowing your assignments had grown and everything had just changed. I had gone to a Bowl game, played LSU. Bert Jones, the great LSU quarterback, came off the bench and threw for three touchdown passes and won the game for them. I was named the Most Valuable Player on Defense. Howard Cosell said I would draft in the first round. That's how I think I got discovered by the NFL.

After that game, I got cards and letters from every NFL team. They sent me stuff like I was going there the next year. But, of course, I had to play my senior year first.

My year as a senior, I was picked as an All-American for every sporting team and the Kodak All-American team had picked me. I went to the *Playboy* mansion, and met Hugh Hefner and the girls. During the last week of practice that year, I went up for an interception and I somehow came down on my leg and I twisted my knee. I ended up damaging some cartilage. I tried to come back for the Colorado game but I wasn't 100 percent, so I ended up re-injuring my knee. I thought Jackie Sherrill was going to take the coach's head off for sending a Colorado player in there for a "cheap shot" block, as he called it, and because of that, I wasn't able to finish the game or season. The team went on to the Liberty Bowl and I wasn't able to play. It was kind of a setback, not being able to play, but also that we lost that game too.

From that point, I could relax a bit, heal, and reflect. A lot of agents came and talk to me during this time—they even brought cash and showed it to me. "If you go now, we'll get you a good spot," they'd all say, but I didn't believe all that. I decided to come back and play again to see if I was ready for the NFL, even though I wasn't really thinking about the NFL. I had my sights on getting my education, then going back to Dayton, Ohio, and being a physical education teacher.

I finished rehabbing my knee, which turned out to be cartilage damage and a stretched ligament. Before the beginning of that year, the NFL had put me down as the first- or second-round draft pick as a linebacker at my position, but I didn't quite stay healthy and my stock went down as a player. So I went back to college and played, trusting that my knee would hold out. After that season, I had the opportunity to be drafted by the Vikings even though my stock was still down a little bit. Still, I was drafted in the second round—the fifty-first player picked in 1974. I had graduated in the winter quarter and I was teaching driver's ed in Iowa and I'm thinking, "This is cool. I'm only two hundred miles away." I figured that if the NFL didn't work, I'd go on and continue teaching. Still, I really wanted to make the team.

Mom always told me not to come home until I was successful and I took that literally. The Vikings also drafted Fred McNeill in the first round and he was a great pick because he was fast. He was from UCLA—a great team organization. He had the skills and had the ability. We came in as number one and number two picks, in the first and second rounds, both linebackers. The year before they had five linebackers and they let one of them go, so I figured they would keep five. Somebody had to go between Fred and me and that made me work harder.

That was one thing that I thought I had—the experience and confidence of playing strong safety. I had the passing game down and I knew where to drop and how to react and that gave me the edge. Fred was the best competitor at trying to make the team. By the time training camp was over with, I had the opportunity to start all the pre-season games. I was coming into replace Roy Winston. To be a Viking, he was the man I had to beat. Roy was in his fourteenth year, and I was in my first year. I just knew that Roy had so much experience and knew how to make plays, and he taught me a lot. The thing about Roy and the team is that they shared their knowledge of playing this game as much as they could and that made the bond that we had as a team just outstanding.

Fred and I competed and, by the end of training camp, they had selected both of us to make the team. We were just too valuable, I guess, to cut and let go. We both made special teams.

On special teams, I excelled as a punt blocker, extra point blocker, field goal blocker, and of course, I have a record for that.

After all those years, I look back at the times and the opportunities that I had that were given to me, and of course, playing in two Super Bowls. You can't take that from me, even though we didn't win them. But to play with the greatest players to ever wear purple and gold—Fran Tarkenton, Chuck Foreman, John Gilliam, Alan Page, Carl Eller, Bill Brown, Mick Tingelhoff—was reward in itself.

Carl and I are on the same side on the ball and with two guys at six-feet-six coming at us, it was kind of hard to do. I learned how to make things happen. If there was one thing that separated myself in my career and made me a better player, it was studying the game plan, studying the technology of how to play a linebacker position. Who do you watch first? Who do you look at first from the tight end of the strong side to the near tackle, to the near back, to the guard, near guard, and then center and off guard? To read all those progressions, those are the things that I think made me a better player. Watching film was definitely a plus. I watched film after film after film. Today it's video; it's a lot quicker. They can fast-forward the video to get to the next play. You can't do that on the old film strip on a 16mm projector. Everything has to be quick, fast . . . let's get it done now!

Outside of that, to be a Viking is also to have a vast appreciation for the fans. Getting out in the community, working with the people and whatever else I did during the off-season meant a lot to me because these are the people you live with in your community. They look at you as a hero while I looked at myself as a normal human, wondering what I would do for a job in the future.

My starting salary was only $30,000. That is something that is hard to fathom when compared to what players are making today. My highest check was $200,000 and that was my last season in 1985. My second highest was somewhere around $85,000. It was a big jump because it was the last year of my contract and that was my extension. I never quibbled about getting a pay raise or arguing that I wasn't getting enough. I didn't hold out. I just wanted to do my job and be a Viking.

After being at your first Super Bowl, you're just eager to go back and be at the next Super Bowl and win. The next one we were in was in Pasadena. We were beating the Raiders all the way through so that hurt a little bit to lose that one. It was the second time around and it was just tough. But again, they can't take that experience of going to the Super Bowl away from you, nor can they take your experience of being in the NFL. Being a walk-on, I never dreamed that I would go that far in my professional career. In fact, this year, the Junior College Association has chosen me to be in the Junior College Football Hall of Fame. And from my junior college, I am the only player to be named as a Junior College Hall of Famer, which is something I am proud of. Out of all the players who have come and gone, I was the one chosen to be named for the Hall of Fame. It's just an outstanding feeling.

What are your memories of training camp?

As a rookie, competing with Fred McNeill, the number-one linebacker picked in 1974, singing the alumni fight song standing on a chair, groups of Vikings fans coming to watch practice, all the food and my attempt of a vegetarian diet—which didn't work—the night bed checks and my roommate getting cut the next morning before practice. After lunch, free veterans (Nate Wright, Paul Krause, Doug Sutherland, Fred McNeill) would play bocce ball against Coach Bud Grant, trainer Fred Zambreletti, and Coach Michael J. Nelson. And of course, I made friends with the head of food service.

I have always been an avid photographer and would work on my photography. In 1976, I had a slideshow of our Super Bowl year of playing the Oakland Raiders. For the show, I used six slide projectors mixed in with movie reels—there were even title credits.

I remember Bud would keep on top of every player's health with the doctor to see who was in shape, injured, etc. Once my resting heart rate was low—47 beats per minute. I asked him if anyone else had a lower resting beat. He told me that Jim Anderson (#56) was in my neighborhood. I'll never forget training camp 1979 when Jim Marshall retired after the '78 season.

Military camp, with Les Steckel, Super Man Steve Jordan won the Condition Contest and he received a car. He cashed it in.

How were you selected to be team captain?

Two weeks of camp had passed before our first pre-season game. One morning practice, during team warm ups, prior to a practice game, Bud called me over and told me that when you go out, get in the middle and lead the exercise drills with Captain Ron Yary. He had picked me as the team captain of Vikings defense in 1979.

To be a Vikings captain, I led by working hard on everything I did physically. I did my talking on the field through my big plays and showing my leadership as a captain. My goal was to have a big play each game. The biggest play of my life is having God lead me in life to help others.

Having had a great career in the NFL, what are your overall thoughts on the business of being a player?

When I interviewed Jim Marshall, he indicated, that in the past, players would come to training camp out of shape and would then work to get into shape for the season to come. Today's players work out in the off-season all year round, and it gives them the opportunity to come better fit into camp with all that training and extra that they go through. He noticed that training camp started maybe with eighty-two people, but by the end of the season with injuries and with people on IR [injured reserve] they may end up with seventy-two people.

The system has changed since back in the day. When you get hurt today, you play through it more than you used to because when you get hurt, you lose your starting job to your backup. Back in the day, the backup would have maybe only 75 percent of the skills the starter does. But today, it's a fine line. The backup is just as good as the starter, so it becomes a matter of who's doing everything right and making the right calls.

During the draft, there are special tests they give the players. They give everyone an MRI. Think about it, you have three hundred and sixty guys trying to make the NFL, and MRIs cost anywhere from $800-$1,200 all depending where you go and the NFL pays for all of that. The trainers have to be just as involved as the scout who finds the player. The trainer has to go through and test these guys physically to make the Vikings squad. Hopefully, they can play and, hopefully, the knee injury they had in college doesn't affect their play if they are drafted by the Vikings.

On another note, some players go through a season and never get hurt, but then some players get hurt in training camp, so the powers that be will want to see what they need to recover, what they need to take, and how long it will take to heal. You always hear some of the players giving credit to some guru who maybe worked them out ten times or told them to take a certain supplement or vitamin as opposed to taking the time and working it out naturally. If it's a new injury, it will take time to heal and some players don't have the discipline to wait. They want to be healed today, right now. Our society wants the quick fix. They don't have the patience anymore that they did in the past. I think that's the difference in our players today and our players in the past. The Jim Marshalls, the Carl Ellers, the Alan Pages . . . those guys had patience. They waited, and they knew each other.

What do you have to say to all the fans reading this book?
To do this book and share some of the great moments of past great players and current players is something I wanted to give to the fans, showing them what it takes to be a Viking. I want them to appreciate how difficult it is to make what we do look so easy on the field, so that when they ask "why did they run this, why did they run that" they'll realize it takes a lot of sweat, a lot of time, a lot of patience, and a lot of teamwork to make a play appear as if it was so easy.

As a kid, I moved around a lot to different bases with my dad being in the Air Force. I was born in Hawaii, moved to Alaska, to Spain, to Idaho, to Texas, Ohio, and Pennsylvania. But here in Minnesota when people ask me why I've stayed, I always say it's because of the people; it's a great place to be. It's about the diehard fans the Vikings are blessed to have.

To write this book and to dedicate a portion of the retail selling price to the Special Olympics kids and give them the opportunity to become an athlete like I got the opportunity to do is a gift I am proud to be a part of.

#55 SCOTT STUDWELL

LINEBACKER   1977-1990

Photo taken 1991

S T A T S

HIGH SCHOOL
Name of School: Harrison High School
Location of School: Evansville, Indiana
Graduation: 1972
Position: Linebacker, Wingback
Jersey number: 34
Height: 6 feet 2 inches
Weight: 205 pounds
40 speed: 4.85 seconds
Coach: Don Watson
Other sports played: Baseball

COLLEGE
Name of School: University of Illinois
Location of School: Champaign, Illinois
Graduation Year: 1977
How long attended: 5 years
Did you graduate? No
Major: Finance, Football
Position: Linebacker, Defensive End,
    Defensive Tackle
Jersey number: 67
Height: 6 feet 2 1/2 inches
Weight: 225–270 pounds
40 speed: 4.85 seconds
Coach: Bob Blackman
Other sports played: None

PRO
Position: Middle Linebacker
Jersey number: 55
Year Drafted: 1977
Draft Round: Ninth
Year Retired: 1990
Height: 6 feet 2 1/2 inches
Weight: 220–250 pounds
40 speed: 4.9 seconds
Coaches: Bud Grant, Les Steckell,
    and Jerry Burns

Compare the Met and the Dome.

Well, you know, I was fortunate enough to come into the league when we were still playing outside. I don't think it was a real conducive atmosphere for the fans from a viewing standpoint, but I think, from an overall perspective, it was an all-day affair for them. They were there early in the morning; they were there until late in the evening. Playing on the grass—at least the painted dirt—was, I think, was a lot more conducive to Minnesota football, as opposed to moving inside to the Dome, but the Dome, obviously, has had it's advantages too. The fact that the noise level is there, you're indoors, you're out in the atmosphere, you're playing in more sterile conditions, but I think we lost some of the home field advantage, to be honest with you, when we moved indoors.

What was your favorite stadium to play in—besides home?

Ah, Lambeau Field. I love playing in that atmosphere. I mean that atmosphere was very similar to ours. The grass was always in pretty good shape. That was probably my second favorite stadium. That and Soldier Field was always a challenge and a lot of fun, but I'd have to say it's Lambeau.

The Vikings have been to four Super Bowls. How does that make you feel that you never got a ring, now that your career is over?

I think that would have been the crowning achievement on my career. For anybody who plays this game, that is the ultimate goal—to get to the Super Bowl and to win it. You can take all the individual accolades, you can take all the longevity, you can take all the money that you made and throw it out the window, but the fact that I'm not walking around with a championship ring on—it hurts, and I think a lot of people who have played this game would tell you the same thing. That's what you play for. It's a privilege to play this game, it's a privilege to make a living at this game, but it boils down to winning championships, and we just didn't get there.

How did you balance your family and your career when you were playing?

Actually, it was great. When I came into the league, I didn't have a family until I was probably thirty years old. I played in the league for seven or eight years before I finally settled down. It gave me the opportunity to spend a lot of time with my kids when they were little. Because when you are playing, you basically have six months off, so you're home a lot, and therefore I had the opportunity to be around them when they were very young; that experience in itself was wonderful. Football was a full-time job, yet I could still spend a lot of time at home in the off-season. It takes you away on occasion, but nowhere near where it does now, so it was a great opportunity to be with my kids.

What were your lowest and your highest salaries?

I came in the league at a minimum of $22,000, and I think my last year I was in the $600,000s.

What's your favorite charity, if you have one?

I used to do quite a bit of charitable work and once I started working in the front office—scouting in particular—I had to kind of disassociate myself with it just because of the time constraints. But when I was playing, I had the opportunity to be involved with a lot of charitable organizations, I think Make-A-Wish is probably at the top of my list.

When you retired, what was your first job and what is your current job now?

I'm the Director of College Scouting. After football, I took about two to three months off and thought about what I wanted to do with the rest of my life. I kept coming back to wanting to stay in the game, somehow, someway. So I was very fortunate that the ownership had just changed hands. Roger Hedrick had just come on board so I went in and had a meeting with Roger and tried to lay out some plans to implement some player programs for the organization, so that really worked out exceptionally well for me. I came on as assistant to the president and did a variety of things. I did a lot of work with the coaches, you know, quality control and then it just evolved into a scouting role, and I've been scouting ever since.

#21   RUFUS BESS

DEFENSIVE BACK   1982-1987

Photo taken 2005

STATS

HIGH SCHOOL

High School: Butler High School

Location of School: Hartsville, South Caro

Graduation Year: 1974

Position: Quarterback, Halfback, Corne
     Back, Safety, Kicker, Punter

Jersey number: 14

Height: 5 feet 9 inches

Weight: 162 pounds

40 speed: 4.6 seconds

Coach: Theodore B. Thomas

Other sports played: Baseball, track. All
     conference Quarterback and Defensiv
     Back senior year; Most Valuable back,
     Most Valuable Player in 1973

COLLEGE

Name of School: South Carolina State
     University

Location of School: Orangeburg, South
     Carolina

Graduation Year: 1979

How long attended: 5 years

Did you graduate? Yes

Degree: B.S. Industrial Technology

Position: Defensive Back and Punt Returner

Jersey number: 21

Height: 5 feet 9 inches

Weight: 177 pounds

40 speed: 4.5 seconds

Coach: Willie Jefferies

Other sports played: None

PRO

Position: Defensive Back, Punt
     Returner, Kick Returner

Jersey number: 21 for Vikings

Free Agent/Other: Yes—1979 for
     Oakland Raiders

Year Retired: 1989

Height: 5 feet 9 inches

Weight: 185 pounds

40 speed: 4.5 seconds

Coaches: Jerry Burns, Les Steckel,
     Bud Grant

Rufus Bess made the team as a walk-on in 1975. He was voted Most Valuable Defensive back in 1978. He won the Sheridan Black College Network All-American honors in 1978, and was named All-Conference Defensive Back in 1978 (MEAC).

What were your lowest and your highest contracts when you played?

My lowest contract had to be my first year with the Raiders, at $23,000, and my highest contract was with the Vikings which was $140,000.

What was the year you retired?

I retired in 1989, but I left the game in 1987.

What is your job now?

My job now is an educator in the Minneapolis Public Schools. I was previously over at North High School and am currently the head football coach over at North High School, but this year I'm over at the Minneapolis Urban League Street Academy.

And your future job will be?

Right now I'm looking to make a change of location—to go out to Bloomington Kennedy and become the Work Coordinator there and also coach football.

When did you decide professional football would be your forte?

Probably in high school. When I was in high school I used to always have a vision and a dream of playing football. I remember going to the library many times looking at *Ebony* and just seeing the number of black players in the NFL—and it was only a handful. And just having the dream of hoping that one day I'd have a chance to be there—to have a chance to put the pants on. After listening to guys in my hometown telling how they enjoyed trying out for the pros, I didn't want to be someone who just tried out— I wanted to be a person who played in the game.

Was going to the library something that you normally would do without thinking about football?

Well, I spent time in the library. We had time to go during class and during my free time I would go and look at people in the magazine. I remember Greg Pruitt of Oklahoma when he was winning the Heisman Trophy, he was on the cover of either *Ebony* or *Jet*. Because I played football every day, when it came time to take care of my studies, every now and then we'd either go to the media center or the library and look up people and past players and see them on TV. I watched the games every Sunday. Back then whoever thought I'd be in Minnesota? I didn't! That was one place I always said I wouldn't go.

Once you became a professional player, how did you balance your family with your football career?

Being the oldest boy in my family, it was a great opportunity for me to be a role model for my brother and sisters because my father died when I was in tenth grade, when I was playing high school football. So for me, it was a way to get to college and set the tone for what I wanted them to be a part of. I think everybody in the family has gone on to college and received college degrees. It's a tribute to my mom that each one of us has continued on to school. As far as my family now, they've been very supportive. I got married at the end of my career. I'm the first guy from my hometown to go on to play professional football so it was really special for my high school in South Carolina to have Rufus Bess in the pros.

Talk about your coaching and how the players fit into your program.

High school coaching has been fun. I got a degree in education and it was something that I fought with about going into the school system to teach school because I said I wanted to coach at a higher level, and as I thought about it and time went on I said, "Well, I got a degree in education. A lot of people have helped me along the way, so why not go in here and do some things to try and give some things back to the community?" It was great for me to have the opportunity to coach at a couple of schools and now, being the head coach at North High School, it's been a wonderful experience. We've had great success over there. I think I've done a good job building the program with the kids, and I've had some very good kids come through. It's fit into my plans very well. It's part of things I'll look back on and say I've had some good players. I've had some great players. I'll feel good about the kind of kids who I've helped go on in life. I teach more than just football. It's more about life in general and to be good young men in the community and society. And it's been a great experience for me.

Are there any kids that you coached who have gone on to be pros?

No, not to the professional level yet. I've got kids playing in college and kids playing in semi-pro football, but nobody's made it to the professional level yet. I do think I've had a few that had a great chance of going to the pros, but I try teach them that it's more than about football, that you have to do the little things in order to be professional, it's not just because you want to be one. There's a lot that goes into becoming a professional athlete and I think I've developed a rapport with a lot of them and I've given them that foundation to understand that you can become a pro, you just gotta keep working.

What are your goals or patterns that you use in your coaching?

I think high school football is such a good reminder of where you came from. I've found that, being a high school coach, there are a lot of little things that I remember doing in high school that I wasn't as good at, but I worked on it in college and I've worked on it in the pros and I found out that it's about technique and skills that you combine until you work those techniques and skills everyday and you find out how much better you become. Kids in high school think they're good, but they don't see the impact of working on those things. You just try to encourage them that, hey, this is what I know worked well for me. It might not work quite as well for you, but we're going to work on it and we're going to try and do these little things that are going to make you refine your skills and technique.

Frank Gilliam, head scout for the Vikings, had mentioned in his interview that you can make a team with speed. Do you agree with that?

I do. I had a lot of speed in high school and have a lot at North High School, and going to Kennedy, I don't know what kind of speed they got, but I know they don't have what North has. I do think you have to have speed on a team but I think with teaching guys how to run, teaching speed, you can teach guys how to become faster in their running. I know it helped me learn how to run properly with track and I use that as a teacher as I run my guys every day. I run them every day because I tell them being in shape is very important to lasting all four quarters.

Did you reach all the goals you wanted to reach at the professional level?

No, but my number-one goal was to make it in the pros. I wanted to make All-Pro, but I think the times when I had the opportunity to, I got injured. But being a role player and being the kind of player that I was to me was most important. I think being a role player and making a contribution to helping the team win and being there for the team—game in and game out—and being instrumental in the success of the team was just as important to me. I just love having had the opportunity to play as long as I did being a free agent. Playing with the great guys I played with on three different teams and building a rapport with them over the years.

What did you like about training camp and what didn't you like about training camp?

Coming out of college, we had tough training camps. For me, it was never a big deal. I always believed that training camp wasn't a place where you go to get in shape—just a place to get better. It was just something I was accustomed to. I think the kind of coach I had in high school, they all had college experience and they all had some slim professional experience and, for me, just to work hard, I think it was me more than anything else. The work ethic was very important. I always trained myself to come in and be in shape and to be ready to play and so, for me going in, it was not a big deal. I guess training camp makes a difference for some. I love the training table. I think most guys do. The camaraderie you build and the level that you get to see guys who are coming in to compete for your positions, made a difference for me. I always had to come in and compete among the top draft picks. None of them ever beat me out. I got waived, but I don't think any of them ever beat me out because not many of them went on to do anything after I got released from the team. So, to me, the competition table and the training table were the best thing next to the camaraderie.

What is your favorite meal?

You know, I'm a southern guy, so I like a lot of soul food. I'm a collard greens and rice guy. I like my chicken. I like my ribs and my sweet potato pie. But the training table, I have to say that all the teams I played for, the Raiders, the Bills, and the Vikings, they all had good tables. But it wasn't until I got to Minnesota that I got to experience frog legs—and I grew up in the south. I thought they were great, and they became the part of the meal that I loved most.

What was the best game you played?

I'd have to say that in '85 game when Bud [Grant] came back. I think I made great contributions to a lot of games, but I do have to say that game in 1985, when Bud made his return after being retired after the Les Steckel era. We played against San Francisco in that first game of the season where I was able to cause three fumbles and recover one, have ten tackles and had an interception. Getting voted *Sports Illustrated* Player of the Week was probably one of the greatest honors.

How many days did it take you to recover after a game like that physically?

I never took that into consideration. I remember times when Bud [Grant] actually made me sit down because I had that separated shoulder and I'm trying to do push-ups with everybody. I was only trying to come out and prepare with the guys because that's how strong I felt about the team. For me, it doesn't take long to recover, as I know my body pretty well. I always knew I could overcome an injury pretty fast. If there was nothing broken, I always believed I could play and I've played with several injuries and just felt that to play with injuries and play with pain was part of the game.

What game was the low point in your career?

It's hard to say. I don't really have any in mind. I remember some games when I probably could have played better or made better plays, but I don't have any games that I can think of where I just didn't make contributions in some aspect of the game—whether it was on special teams or as a defensive player. I think back to Oakland, and I think back to Buffalo, and there was a game I can remember in Buffalo where I got beat on two touchdown passes, and I felt I was in great coverage but the guy made a heck of a catch. Cincinnati won the game and they went on to play in the Super Bowl that year. I didn't think I played bad in that game at all and it wasn't just my play that caused us not to win the game. I was in double coverage at the time and I just thought the guy made a heck of a catch. I didn't think the ball was catchable, but he did. But as far as an overall game, I just don't see any that I feel I played terrible or played so bad where I'm going to beat my head against a wall because I always understand it's a game. I may critique it or I maybe get criticized for it, but I don't think there's a game where

I can say that I played so bad that I wasn't ready to come out and play the next game.

Name some of your teammates you played with so people know what era you're in.

I can probably name a few of players on both sides of the ball, but I'll try and be brief with it. Going back to Oakland, being with the Raiders as a free agent in 1979, having the opportunity to play with Lester Hayes, and being a backup to Lester Hayes, played in the secondary with Lester, Jack Tatum, Mike Davis, Charles Philips, Monte Jackson, and those guys. Then you take the defensive line where you have defensive linebackers, Ted Hendricks, Otis Sistrunk, offense you had Gene Upshaw, Art Shell, Ken Stabler, Dave Casper, Raymond Chester. You go to Buffalo and I played with Ron Jessie, Reggie McKenzie. Mario Clark was a defensive back with me. Billy Simpson, Charlie Roams, and then the linebackers Jim Haslet, Fred Murlis. On the offensive line, Joe Ferguson, Joe Cribbs, you take Frank Lewis. Then I came to Minnesota, and I got you, Matt, and then there was John Turner, Joey Browner, Carl Lee, Scott Studwell, Mark Mullaney. You got Tommy Kramer, Ted Brown, Sammy White, Ahmad Rashad, just a group of great guys who I admire and had the opportunity to play with. Hell, I always tell people if I don't make the Hall of Fame, I'm with the Hall of Fame crew. I always say I got Hall of Famers on every team I ever played for. So it's just a great relationship, and I think a lot of time that's what I got out of the game. I love team camaraderie and the opportunity to be around the guys who I had the chance to play with.

What is your favorite charity?

Well, I like a lot of charities. I do a lot for the United Way. The Multiple Sclerosis Society is another. I have a brother-in-law who has Multiple Sclerosis. I would love to be more involved with sickle-cell anemia. My father died of sickle-cell anemia and that's one that I really would like to start doing more for. Others like heart disease and diabetes. There's a variety of charities I've done things for and continue to do things for—anything to do with kids and giving them awareness.

What advice would you give kids who have aspirations of becoming a professional player?

I always tell them to do the very best they can. To go out and give their best efforts and, when you feel you've done your best, and you still don't come out on top, don't feel bad because you've done the best that you can and you move on. You know, just strive hard to achieve excellence in every way you can and always understand that it's a game and sometimes things are going to go well and sometimes things aren't going to go so well. But make sure you strive hard to get an education. Get a degree and move on from there.

#47 JOEY BROWNER

DEFENSIVE BACK 1983-1991

Photo taken 2005

STATS

HIGH SCHOOL
Name of School: Southwest High School
Location of School: Atlanta, Georgia
Graduation Year: 1979
Position: Defensive End and Tight End
Jersey number: 89
Height: 6 feet 3 inches
Weight: 195 pounds
40 speed: 4.4 seconds
Coach: Coach Turman
Other sports played: Basketball, track, and
karate

COLLEGE
Name of School: University of Southern
California
Location of School: Los Angeles, California
Graduation Year: 1983
How long attended: Four years
Did you graduate? No
Major: Public Administration
Position: Corner Back and Safety
Jersey number: 47
Height: 6 feet 3 inches
Weight: 200 pounds
40 speed: 4.4 seconds
Coach: John Robinson
Other sports played: None

PRO
Position: Corner Safety
Jersey number: 47
Year Drafted: 1983
Draft Round: First
Year Retired: 1996
Height: 6 feet 3 inches
Weight: 210 pounds
40 speed: 4.5 safety
Coach: Bud Grant, Jerry Burns

Do you prefer a turf or grass playing field?

I prefer grass because there are fewer injuries. It's natural for me to say that, I played my college and my high school—most of my high school career—on grass, so I really prefer playing on grass.

What was your favorite game with the Minnesota Vikings?

Well, I have two. My favorite games were when I played in '85 and my brother Keith was playing for the Tampa Bay Buccaneers. My mother was able to see that game. And then also my brother Ross played for the Cincinnati Bengals and my mother was able to see that game. So those were my two favorite games.

What was your lowest and highest contract amount?

Lowest was about $50,000 and the highest was like $600,000. I think it was $600,000 or $700,000.

How many autographs do you think you've signed over the years?

Oh, that's a good question. I think I could win the presidency with all the autographs I've signed.

What are your thoughts regarding players being interviewed by women in the locker room?

Well, it was difficult at first because the first time I ran into the incident was in Los Angeles at the Coliseum at a college game. I guess a reporter is a reporter. I think it's not fair that there you are in a situation that's very compromising and, you know, a woman is there being able to interview you and, well, there's a comprising situation. I just think that it's best for them to be outside the locker room instead of inside the locker room.

Do you have anything to add to your Vikings or NFL career?

To get a chance to get into the Hall of Fame—that's the only thing I'd like to add to it. Other than that, it's been a blessing to have an opportunity to play the number of years I did in the NFL.

What advice would you give to young kids coming up in sports?

Enjoy the sports while you can when you're young. Once you get to college and play the sport, get your education because that's something that you can take with you and be able to maximize yourself on. If you get an opportunity to play in the pros, it's like hitting the lottery because there's like over ten thousand kids from each position who graduate every year, and you gotta get really lucky to get into it. So enjoy it while you can and get an education and get a job. Because when you're looking at the dream, it only comes around once and if you can't get that dream, always have your main dream in life foremost and that's what your career is going to be.

Playing in your time and playing today, what do you think about it and how do you compare the two?

I just feel that when I came into the league in '83 and played against the players who were from the '70s and the '60s during that time, it was all about the game. And I just feel that when I came into the league the arms were not extended, they were still retracted for offensive linemen and they were still allowed to hit people, make tackles, and you were allowed to cover the wide receivers and jam them all up and down the field. As time progressed, it just took away from the players going at it mano-a-mano; you couldn't play man for man, you couldn't go out and dominate your opponent. Now, over the last twenty years, it's gotten to where players can't tackle one another—they can't get out there and get after one another. And if you hit the quarterback now, you get fined for just hitting him. So even for just making a tackle you get fined. It's just taken away from how the game was actually played. But then, too, the players are really arrogant;

they're pompous. They don't care about anybody. They don't care about the community. They don't care about the team. They're just me, me, me, and I, I, I. And I think that's the worst part of the game—that it's come down to the money. Nothing wrong with making the money. I'm not mad at the kids or anything, but why don't they go out there and play the game like it used to be played. And we'll really see what kind of athletes we have.

#26 ANTOINE WINFIELD

DEFENSIVE BACK 2004-PRESENT

Photo taken 2005

S T A T S

HIGH SCHOOL
Name of School: Garfield High
Location of School: Akron, Ohio
Graduation Year: 1995
Position: Running Back and Free Safety
Jersey number: 24
Height: 5 feet 9 inches
Weight: 185 pounds
40 speed: 4.5 seconds
Coach: Bill McGhee
Other sports played: None

COLLEGE
Name of School: Ohio State University
Location of School: Columbus, Ohio
How long attended: 1995-1999
Did you graduate? No
Position: Corner Back
Jersey number: 11
Height: 5 feet 9 inches
Weight: 180 pounds
40 speed: 4.4 seconds
Coach: John Cooper
Other sports played: None

PRO
Position: Corner Back
Jersey number: 26
Year Drafted: 1999
Draft Round: First
Height: 5 feet 9 inches
Weight: 180 pounds
40 speed: 4.4 seconds
Coach: Mike Tice

What was your first day with the Vikings at training camp like?

I was excited. I just signed a nice-sized deal and I felt I had to get out there and prove myself before I came out all vocal. I didn't want to come out and step on anyone's toes. I knew a lot of the players like Randy [Moss] and Daunte [Culpepper]. I talked to them, like right before the season, so the first day, I was just excited to be here.

Now that you've had experience with the team, what are your likes or dislikes about training camp?

Well there's not much to like about training camp. Imagine getting up early in the morning and working out twice a day and it's hot. On the other hand, being around the team among the guys in the locker room is cool. I guess when you're tired, you miss that— just the camaraderie of being around them and having fun.

What day of the week is your favorite day during the season?

Sundays. I love playing the game. I love competing. I'm a very competitive guy. I hate to lose. So Sunday—that's my favorite day.

What makes you stand out from the other players? Is it practice or is it watching film that makes you the player that you are?

More film study. I pride myself on going in and watching a lot of film. I try to get an advantage doing that. It's hard to do that and guess the receivers' routes, so I go in there and study receivers' tendencies, see what they're good at, what they're not good at—see if they're good getting off the press.

Was studying film something you started in college?

Yes. I was fortunate that I had veterans in front of me. I had Sean Springs and Ty Howard. When I got to the house, they told me that was real important. To go in there and study your opponent because that's the only way you can get the advantage. You can't just go out there like I said and just guess routes or you'll get embarrassed on Sundays.

Are you a person who sets goals?

You have to set goals. I set certain goals that are attainable, but still I set some that are very high that I want to reach—like leading the league in interceptions. I want to make it to the Pro Bowl, win a Super Bowl before I retire, and things like that. I haven't hit any of them yet, but hopefully, I will.

Do you have any goals for the 2005 season?

Yes. Number one is to make it to the Pro Bowl. I'm going on my 7th year and I'm playing up to the standards that I need to play in. Two is to try and lead the league in interceptions, stay healthy, try to get my team better—to finish number one as a secondary and as a defense. And try and win that ring.

You were definitely a dominant corner for the Vikings last year. How will you use your experience to help them become a better team?

That's always a tough thing when you have other guys coming in to a new team. You have to get that camaraderie. Darrin Sharper and I were just talking about going in next week and start studying film together. You want to get on the same page and I think you do that by studying film and mini-camps always helps, so by the time the season starts, we'll all be ready to go.

How does family work into your career? Who comes first?

Family is very important. You always have to put family first because they're always going to be there. I mean, football only lasts a few years, and I'll be done, but I always try to spend as much time with my family as possible. Even with the long work days that we have, I still make time to go home and play with my kids and help them with their homework or whatever and put them to bed. Then I study my film, but I always put them first.

Do you have a favorite charity?

Not exactly, no. I don't have a charity, I just have a football camp that I do in Akron every year in June, but a charity, no. I don't have one.

When you get to a situation on the team that you can't handle, is there anybody that you turn to—on or off the team?

Well, I talk to my wife a lot. She knows me better than anyone in the world. And if it's not her, it's my mom. I turn to her and we talk a lot. She knows a lot about the game so when I'm out there, she'll say, "You're lagging!" or "You're not playing hard enough!" She keeps me on my toes.

What was your first pay as a rookie?

My signing bonus was for over $3.5 million.

#42 DARREN SHARPER

DEFENSIVE BACK 2005-PRESENT

Photo taken 2005

STATS

HIGH SCHOOL
Name of School: Hermitage High School
Location of School: Richmond, Virginia
Graduation Year: 1993
Position: Quarterback
Jersey number: 2
Height: 6 feet 1 inch
Weight: 185 pounds
40 speed: 4.6 seconds
Coach: Gus Allen
Other sports played: Basketball, track

COLLEGE
Name of School: College of William and Mary
Location of School: Williamsburg, Virginia
Graduation Year: 1997
How long attended: Four years
Did you graduate? Yes
Degree: Sociology
Position: Defensive Back
Jersey number: 12
Height: 6 feet 2 inches
Weight: 210 pounds
40 speed: 4.4 seconds
Coach: Jimmy Laycock
Other sports played: None

PRO
Position: Cornerback, Safety
Jersey number: 42
Year Drafted: 1997
Draft Round: Second
Height: 6 feet 2 inches
Weight: 208 pounds
40 speed: 4.3 seconds
Coach: Mike Holmgren, Ray Rhodes,
    Mike Sherman, Mike Tice

First of all, how does it feel to be a Viking?

It feels good to be with older guys who I actually played against eight years of my career with Green Bay when it was us always battling them for the division. The Vikings are a good organization, a winning organization, and I hope I can come in and contribute to that and hopefully get to the Super Bowl. One of my aspirations, definitely, before my career is over with is to win a Super Bowl and I think this is one of organizations I have a chance to do that with.

How big of a thorn were the Vikings to Green Bay?

They were definitely a big thorn—especially against Chris Carter, Jake Reed, and Randy Moss. Those three were thorns in my side because I was always going against them. Then came Daunte Culpepper, you know. He was always tough to go against. The Vikings were one of the rivals in our division where you knew it was going to be a tough, tough game. You always had to come and bring your best because it was really one of those NFC North grudge matches that you knew was going to be real physical and you had to play your butt off to win. You knew every game was going to be close.

When did you start thinking about football as a kid?

I first started playing in fourth grade for little league—for Junior Randolph recreational league which was about a mile up from where I grew up. All my friends played there. We played basketball, we played football there. You want to be with your friends, and that's where I started thinking about football.

Were you and your brother on the same team in high school?

He is a year older than I am, but we were on the same team pretty much growing up. I wouldn't necessarily say we were beating up on everybody because we were pretty much not spectacular athletes. We were average athletes, we were good, but no one was necessarily looking at it like "those kids will be playing in the NFL one day." We were just playing football and that's just about it. But as we grew and got older, we started dominating people we played against.

Were you and your brother the only professional athletes in your family?

My father actually played with Kansas City. He got to camp and got hurt after a year, then we had to come home to take care of my sister who was born right around that time, so he kind of left his dreams of playing in the NFL. But yeah, my brother, Jamie Sharper, number 55 for the Seattle Seahawks, and I are the only ones in my immediate family to make it to the NFL.

When you were in high school, how vast were your college choices?

My choices were pretty limited. In high school, I played quarterback and I was about maybe six foot, maybe six-one and 180 pounds. I didn't play too much defense. I was a decent quarterback. I got banged up a little bit my senior year, but my stats didn't end up being as spectacular as I'd have liked them to be. So I didn't get offered by too many big name schools. I really went to college to think about my education and that's why I decided to go to William and Mary.

What career would you be doing now had you not gone to the NFL?

I majored in sociology. Had I not made it to the NFL, I'd have gone back and gotten my master's degree in criminal justice. Before I was drafted in my senior year, I met with an FBI agent and found out what was necessary to get into the FBI, so I was going to go back to school and get a criminal justice degree with hopes to get into the FBI.

What do you think contributes to you being the athlete you are?

The main thing was just timing. When I graduated from high school, I could barely dunk a basketball. As soon as I stepped on the college campus, I don't know what it was, I could do whatever I wanted on the basketball court—dunking or whatever, it was like my body just matured that year, and it showed true even after college. When I went to the combine my senior year, I looked around at different guys that I was measuring up athletic ability, and mine was always at the top. In high school, I would have never predicted that. I think that my body was a late bloomer which allowed me to do that. So it was in me, it just took a while for it to come out.

Being a late bloomer, you probably thought about the professional side of it a little bit later into your college career?

Yeah, I definitely did. After my junior year, a scout came in and sat down and told me what I needed to do to make it to the next level. He basically told me I needed to dominate, and dominate on the level. I played on the one AA level, and I needed to show all the scouts I was dominating that level and could compete against anyone who I was playing against. That was my goal my senior year and I really just stepped it up. It really paid off.

Were there any other players in your school system that came out the same time?

We had a couple other players who were a year behind me who had a good chance to get to the pros. We had a quarterback who had a chance, he actually was in camp. A linebacker who actually came behind me, Drew Waddy. He played for two years with me, so there were a couple guys who had the opportunity. I think I hopefully opened up a couple doors for them once I got to the NFL because we still have players from my school who are still getting opportunities because scouts are going back down to check them out.

How did it feel to be on a team with those key players in the Green Bay Packers?

Having the opportunity to play with the late Reggie White, Bret Favre, Antonio Freeman, Gilbert Brown, Santana Dotson, LeRoy Butler, all guys whose names are leaders in this league really allowed me to learn something from playing with them, but also taught me things that I needed to do off the field to perform at a higher level. It was a blessing, especially my rookie year, to play with all those great players and learn from them. It let me have the production and the success I've had so far in my career. So I really came from a good situation and a great organization.

Now being with the Vikings for a short period, who are some of the guys who are kind of leading the way for you and showing you what to do?

Well, being a veteran, I pretty much know what I need to do as far as coming in and working out. But most of the guys I've known because I've been around the league. Of course I know Daunte [Culpepper]; I played in the Pro Bowls with him. I also know Michael Bennett, who was in the Pro Bowl with me. Other guys who I played against, who would always try to smack me around and get cheap shots—Marcus Robinson and Nate Burleson— were big thorns in my side last year in Green Bay. So I know a couple of the guys and for the others I just tried to get a different feel of people around the organization. They definitely have been a great help to me, and all the guys on the team seem to be great guys and you can really see that this team is a close knit group, similar to what we had in Green Bay.

What are your expectations for the 2005 season? Do you feel with all the trades and acquisitions going on that we have the team to make it all the way this year?

Definitely. I know our defense has the makings of being a top five defense. Not just top ten, but a top five defense in the league. We know our offense is going to be top five because of the talent we have and the guy we have pulling the trigger. Put all that together in addition to special teams, and we have the chance to go far. You know, everyone expects Philadelphia and Atlanta to be there in the end and now they're also expecting us to be there in the end. I definitely think we have the team to represent the NFC in the Super Bowl this year.

Do you have any goals set for this year besides winning the Super Bowl?
No. That's it. That's it, man.

What's your favorite food?
Oh man, I have a couple of them. I love a great steak. A great well seasoned, tender steak is probably one of the best things I love to eat. But besides that, I'm a big seafood fan.

Do you have a career planned after the NFL?
One thing that I definitely want to do is stay around the game. I want to get into broadcasting; maybe broadcast games for NFL-Europe.

What advice do you have for kids with aspirations of making it to the NFL?
One thing I always tell kids is that when you set your goals, set them so you can do everything you can to attain them. Always be well rounded in your goals. Never lose sight of the things that will allow you to do that. Be good at school and get good grades because if you don't perform well at school, it will not allow you to go to college. If you decide you want to do something, do everything in your power to accomplish them because the good man upstairs gives everyone the talent, but it's up to you to find out what that talent is and to do everything possible to achieve that talent.

#2 DARREN BENNETT

SPECIAL TEAMS 2004-PRESENT

Photo taken 2005

S T A T S

PRO
Position: Punter
Number: 2
Height: 6 feet 5 inches
Weight: 235 Pounds
Coach: Mike Tice

Interview taped at Winter Park, Eden Prairie, Minnesota, July 2005

Being From Australia, how did you get into American football?

I played Australian rules football growing up and I played professionally for twelve seasons. I retired in 1993 and came across on my honeymoon with my wife. I had a mutual friend who knew some people around the NFL and was lucky enough to get a tryout with the San Diego Chargers. I stuck with them in '94—the year they went to the Super Bowl. I was on the practice squad that year and then, fortunately enough, spent a year in the World League in Amsterdam and came back and got the starting job in '95. So, up until I came here with the Vikings last year, I was in San Diego.

In Australia, were you a kicker? Did you start in high school?

I played Junior Australian rules football, so in Aussie rules, it's a totally different game to American football, but we kick the ball everywhere. So the skills that I learned in Aussie rules are sort of translated across to the punting game here. I have a young son who is seven years old who has been kicking around a football since he was three or four. We learned how to kick a ball before we learned how to throw it. It was the one skill that I could transfer across to the American game. I never wore helmet or shoulder pads. My first game with the Chargers was my first game in a helmet.

How did it feel with all the gear on?

It took a little while to get the parameters of holding the ball in the same spot as when you don't have pads on. I was fortunate enough that, you know, spending the year on the practice squad was great for me because it allowed me to get used to the pads, get used to the helmets, take input from our equipment guys on what the best way to wear them was and how tight they had to be and all that sort of stuff. I think about being thrown in the first year as an active player and I probably wouldn't have handled it very well, so I was thankful for that.

How far was your longest punt here in the United States?

In a game I punted 66 yards. I've done that about fourteen times. For some reason I can't get it to 67, but 66 is well far enough. The guys are going to cover it at 65 yards. They're not too happy about it, so I try to get them somewhere in the fifties or as high as I possibly can.

You're a pretty big size for a punter, right?

Yeah, I'm a bit bigger than I started, too. I grew a little bit each year as I got older too, but there's a trend toward taller punters in the league now. When I first came in, it was basically myself and Matt Turk—we were about 6 feet 5 inches. Maybe Mark Royals is that tall as well. But the trend is toward bigger guys now.

Is that because of the way the defense is set up? Meaning bigger guys are taller and stronger to punt the ball?

I'm not really sure. As I'm saying that, there are not as many guys coming into the league. I think it's a coincidence. I think it's a generational thing, every generation is getting larger. You look at the linemen, they're getting larger than when I first came in. I think everyone's getting a bit bigger.

Do speed and strength play a factor for a punter in the NFL these days?

I think leg speed plays a big factor but mainly it's flexibility and consistency. I'm no where near as athletic as when I first started. I think it's not really a prerequisite, it's probably for once or twice a year when a returner breaks loose, your athleticism comes in. I think they'd rather take an unathletic punter who can be consistent than a very athletic one who can't be consistent.

Does Kurtis [Shultz], the athletic trainer for the Vikings, give you a certain amount of exercises specific to a kicker?

I think I even have a different program from the young kickers. Kurtis has given me a great amount of scope to do what I've always done, which is basically ride and bike and I do a lot of flexibility stuff. I try to keep my core strong, but I really don't do as much running and lifting as the younger guys. I find it sort of tightens me up a little bit and I like to try and stay as flexible as possible. To his credit, Coach Tice, Kurtis, and Rusty Gillman [the special teams coach for the Vikings] got together and said let's let him do what he does well. For me, riding the bike gives me the leg speed with the strength and keeps my hip flexors nice and strong. Knock-on-wood, I've only had one injury in twelve years and that was making a tackle, so hopefully we can keep that going this year.

How many tackles have you made in your career?

There were a couple years there, I was making three or four a year, but not as much lately. Especially in the past couple years. Last year was the credit of our coverage. I never got within forty yards of the punt returner, you know? We were fantastic in not allowing big returns. I think we were one of the few teams that didn't allow big returns. There were a couple years in the middle where I was making two or three a year. I'm sort of happy I don't have to do it. I'd rather the big fellas do it!

With the acquisition with all the new players, do you think the Vikings team this year is going to be special?

I think every year Coach Tice has been the head coach, he's made strides to making the team he strives to have. This year, I think we've made a quantum leap. Hopefully, we stay healthy. That's the big thing in the NFL, and that's to stay healthy the whole season. Sometimes, it's the team that has the least injuries that gets all the way through, and I think if we stay healthy and get Matt Birk back after his surgery, I think we're really going to be a formidable team.

Can you give an idea of what your day of practice is like as a kicker?

Normally, I'll warm up with the team. All our kickers warm up, then we find a gap somewhere in there to go and kick some field goals. Today was a shorter practice, but we had punt returns, so in between the first punt session and the second punt session, we went and kicked field goals for 25-30 minutes. So normally, I have to have 10-15 minutes for me to warm up which is what we had today for the second period. And then basically, I'll do some technique stuff. A bit of flexibility and then I'll ride the bike to keep the legs going. I find that if you just stand on the sideline for half and hour after kicking, you stiffen up. I prefer to keep the legs rolling and just sit on the bike and keep a little bit of mobility there. Plus it breaks up the boredom of standing in the same place on the field, or you can get run over by a big fella, so I'd rather be over near the bikes away from everybody else. If they need us, we come in and hold for field goals and extra points.

If you're needed to hold for a field goal and not punt, is that a hard thing for you?

No. There's always been games, obviously I punted a bit more in San Diego than I do here, and that took me a little while to get used to last year, you know having one punt every game and not knowing. You may warm up at 11:00 or something and not have your first punt until 2:45. So that's a difficult thing, especially in cold weather. I think the adrenaline of the game takes over and keeps you warmed up a little bit more than you'd usually be. I have a set regime everytime we get onto offense. You know, I'll go and hit some punts in the net and then I'll take some snaps. So you're always constantly, mentally working as well and the game seems to fly past you. You try and do the same thing every time so you don't get surprised by anything—if we don't punt or if we do punt. I have that regime set together so that we stretch and hit a few punts. We do the same thing every time.

What do you think makes the difference between those who make the team and those who don't make the team?

I think that certain positions that were a quantum leap from college to the NFL are not there anymore. I think a lot of the great college programs pretty much practice almost like we do. And they develop these young men into athletes and very mature athletes at a very young age. I think the mental side of it is the big leap and some players can't make that mental leap. Every year you see great athletes come in training camp. You know, Mike Tice is one of these coaches who will keep you if he thinks you are NFL caliber. And so he cuts good players every year, and every coach probably has to go through the same thing. He promises guys that if they are good on special teams and are good at their position, he'll find a way to keep you. I think that's the thing. You have such great physical players coming out of college now but it comes down to the mental side of it. They throw so much more at them in a playbook and their recognition has to be a lot higher than in college. And some players can't make that adjustment and some players make that adjustment fairly easily.

What advice would you give a kid who is trying to get out there, trying to be an athlete, trying to go to the next level?

We all have dreams in life and I'm living proof that you can dream something and make it happen. No goal is unachievable. I would say that you always have to look at your strengths and look at your determination to do something. And be very honest with yourself. If you are four-foot-eleven it's pretty hard to be an offensive lineman. But you can definitely be a kicker or something like that. Once you set your goals and set them high, make a plan and stick to your plan, that's something that I've always lived by. I always try to formulate a plan on how I'm going to do something and then go ahead and try and execute it. And the other thing is, and not necessarily just for football, but anything in life. You look at all the cool things and all the hard things in life and someone makes a living doing it. So if you have a passion in life, not necessarily for sport but for anything, the same thing applies. You set your goals high and you try and achieve it. If you achieve those first goals, then you reset those goals and you go ahead and do it again. The sky's the limit. I always say that the person who ended as a president, started as a child. So you have to have aspirations somewhere.

THE COACHES

BUD GRANT

HEAD COACH   1967-1983, 1985

Photo taken 1976

HIGH SCHOOL
Name of School: Superior Central High
    School
Location of School: Superior, Wisconsin
Graduation Year: 1945
Position: End, Free Safety, and Linebacker
Number: 13
Height: 6 feet 3 inches
Weight: 195 pounds
Coach: Harry Conley
Other sports played: Basketball, baseball

COLLEGE
Name of School: University of Minnesota
Location of School: Minneapolis, Minnesota
Graduation Year: 1949
How long attended: 4 years
Did you graduate? No
Position: End Linebacker
Number: 13
Height: 6 feet 3 inches
Weight: 200 pounds
Coach: Bernie Bermaine
Other sports played: Basketball, baseball

PRO
Position: Defensive End, Linebacker,
    Safety, and Corner
Number: 83-86
Year Drafted: 1950
Draft Round: First—twelfth player taken
Year Retired: 1956
Height: 6 feet 3 inches
Weight: 205 pounds
Coach: Allen Sherman

What is the comparison between when you coached the Vikings, and the players today?

Players are better today, and they get better every year. The reasons are that I think there are more players who aspire to become professional football players than years ago. There's a greater selection, and I think younger players at an early age decide, "Well, I'm going to play in high school, college, and I want to be in pro football." I want to be "like Mike" kind of attitude. So anyway, that's all weeded out. Today you start with a much bigger base and selection process. The coaches recognize the talented and they get guys on weight programs where it's not uncommon to get players weighing 275-300 pounds in high school nowadays; you didn't see that many years ago. So there's a greater well of players to draw from and that's why we have thirty-two teams in the National Football League that can supply all those teams to play at a high level. And the skill level, I think if you look back at how many 300 pounders we had when I was drafting, and how many 300 pounders come out of college today and there's no comparison. You look at the teams that we had when offensive linemen where 200-250 pound range, and now, if you're not 300 pounds, you might not get a shot. So the players' skills are better and training is better and if you get after it at an earlier age, overall football is better.

Your schedule for the players when you coached the Vikings, you didn't have them meet all the time. You didn't have them workout all the time. Was there a reason for that?

I think it's important to be self motivated for whatever reason. It could be monetarily, it could be ego, which is big in the entertainment business and is a very strong motivator. You want to make a living; all those things can make you motivated to be as good as you can. And if you get a team that is basically self-motivated, I don't have to be on you to go lift every other day, we don't have to take you to a camp to evaluate you because I've had you for 3, 4, 5, 6, 8, 10, 12, 14, 18, 19 years. So there's no necessity to do that. With today's squads, every team in the National Football League has a 50 percent turnover. With free agency, salary cap, every team every year has 50 percent different players. And top players change around, so they have to evaluate and maybe get them in the right scheme of things; we didn't have to do that. Our team was half a dozen players a year, which we'd get out of the draft, primarily. A few trades were thrown in, but we didn't have to do that. Once you get a nucleus of players who understood they had to report to training camp in shape, we didn't have to worry about spending a lot of extra time. We could refine conditioning in training camp, which was longer than it is today, by the way. So there was not the need, once you know your players. I was talking to Mike Tice the other day and I was telling him, "You have 50 percent. Every year you have to evaluate and put them in the proper slots," so I said I would have a difficult time because we worked under a different system than they do today.

What was your proudest moment as a head coach with the Vikings?

The thing I'm proudest of is I didn't get fired! That's the most important thing. In my entire coaching career, I've only been two places and that was Winnipeg and here. And I wouldn't have gone anyplace else from Winnipeg because that was a very good experience. The only other place I would have gone was to the Vikings; I wouldn't have gone to San Francisco or Miami or Atlanta. Basically, my incentive to be a coach was to provide for six kids and a family. Well, this was the best place to do it.

As far as a proudest moment, there are so many games that you go through the emotions of winning or losing. I don't think you can have a best or you can have a favorite. It's a sum and total of what they've all done and you are grateful for what they've done. I think there are favorite players and favorite games at different times—I don't think I can answer that question.

Was there a game that stood out that you were happy to say that you beat another team?

I think coming from Canada where I coached and accepting the job here which had been offered previously, I kept asking myself the question; "Well, am I good enough to coach in this league?" The first game we won was against Green Bay down in Milwaukee against Lombardi and a Packer team that was really good and we won on a close score. I can't remember if it was 13-7, 13-6 or whatever it was. But winning the first game, against a good football team, I thought "well, maybe I can do this in this league." That was a memorable game and of course, it went on from there.

After appearing in four Super Bowls, is there any advice that you can give to future players and coaches? And is there anything you can add to the present team?

I can only answer that by saying that if we had won four Super Bowls, I wouldn't be doing anything else. I'd be doing exactly what I've been doing ever since I've been here. The one thing you've got to remember about football is that it's entertainment. There aren't a lot of residuals to winning. You may get a better contract, you may get a bonus for winning, but sport is entertainment. It provides entertainment for people but there's not much left after the game. I mean there's nothing after the morning newspaper. You throw that away, who can remember what happened last week, and last week, and last week. I don't look back and say, "If we had done this, or if we had done that . . ." This is not a looking back job. You've got to look forward. I don't care whether you look back on a win and feel good or you look back on a loss and feel bad. I think I'm as competitive as the next person in anything you do, but it's not a backward-looking situation. We did the best we could. That's why it's called the Super Bowl; it's one game, winner take all. If we had played a Stanley Cup or something, or a World Series or NBA playoff, we'd have come back the next day and beat any one of those teams—or maybe one three-out-of-five or four-out-of-five—but we don't do that. That's why it's called the Super Bowl. One game. You give it your best shot. You know the football is a funny shape, it's not a round ball, it's a goofy looking ball that takes funny bounces and you can go back and say if we'd have done this or we would have done that. I may have grey hair from coaching, but I've got my health. I can't look back and think what could have happened.

Saturday was a special day during the season. You'd have practice and you'd go out after that and hunt. Can you elaborate on that?

Well, we always practiced all day Saturday before a home game, and on Saturday morning before an away game. When I first came into the league, we would practice Saturday afternoon at the site we were gong to play on Sunday. Well, I changed that quickly. That made no sense to me. So we practiced before we left on Saturday morning and then when we started flying to away games we didn't have to leave until noon in most places. One thing, coaching is an all encompassing job. You work seven days a week, but I still had a family, and I like the outdoors and the only chance I had to go outdoors was on a Saturday afternoon when we had a home game. So I'd say, "Well, we'd like to practice early Saturday morning" so you'd get in the routine of getting up early on Sunday morning to go to a game. Well, that was kind of a façade. It would allow us to practice early so we'd get off early. I've got four boys who liked to hunt, so we'd go hunting close to the cities. Again, we didn't ever get a lot, but it would give us a chance to maintain a family relationship with sons and daughters that a lot of football coaches don't have. I remember two incidents. John Madden, one time, was telling me he came home and his wife said, "Great. Now you can be home for Johnny's birthday. He said, "Oh, how old is he going to be, twelve?"

"No, he's going to be fourteen."

So not only did he lose track of his kid's birthday, but he lost track of how old he was. That was one of the reasons he got out of coaching. Another was Lombardi's son, who worked at the League office and then worked at St. Thomas, so I got to know him because he was in the league. He'd go a whole football season and never talk to his dad. He'd be so involved. Well, I didn't want to become that kind of an animal. So I made sure to make a point that I not only had time for my wife, but my kids. I'd know when their birthdays were and how old they were.

What was the finest day in your career? Was it being inducted into the Hall of Fame?

That's something I really didn't spend a lot of time thinking about. I really didn't feel it, until it happened. When it happened, we visited the Hall of Fame, we played at Canton games, so I'd been at the Hall. We had two people from my hometown, Superior, Wisconsin, who were in the Hall of Fame early on. But it really didn't dawn on me what an honor it was until after I'd been inducted and after I went through all the hoopla that goes with the Hall of Fame. It was only after that when I really felt honored because I really hadn't planned or thought much about it. It was something that I made no attempt, no effort to get into the Hall of Fame. But now that I'm in it, I'm very proud. I'm honored to be in it with that group of players, and that group of coaches and the Hall of Fame people who I've met since. And it's a remarkable place and quite an honor.

Over the years, is there one season's team that you're most proud or disappointed by?

Every team, even though we didn't have a lot of turnover of people, had a character of it's own. The tough part of being on top was that even though we were in the playoffs almost every year, most of the teams ended up losing their last games. It can kind of leave a bad taste in your mouth if you let it. But we had good teams and good times and we earned our money. I recall we lost to Dallas at home on that Drew Pearson push off, which was a great move on his part, by the way, but he's a basketball player. We can understand how he did that. He pushed down on the hip and . . . anyhow, that team was probably as good a team as we had. If that play had not happened, we'd probably look back on that series before that when we marched the length of the field with five minutes to go, or six minutes to go, from our 20 down to Dallas and scored a touchdown. We were about as dominant as we could be and I'm sure had that game ended differently, we'd have beat Denver in Super Bowl that year. But if there was one disappointing moment, that was part of it; Pearson making a great play, as players do, and then the officiating prior to that made two errors on an out of bounds play—those are the things that bother you. It's not the players making plays; it's the officiating either making or not making plays that bothered me more than anything else. That was maybe our most dominant team. We were always in the playoffs.

Do you think the officials should go to school or have a school set up for them?

I think they should be fulltime, yeah. They should be fulltime officials. It's cost me a lot of money to publicly state that, but they should. You know, it would be hard for you to drive a country road all day and end up on a freeway on Sunday. And that's what they do. I mean they look at some film and then all of a sudden it's Sunday afternoon, this is the game. The game has gotten so fast and so intricate that they have a tough time. I sympathize with them but I know that if you watch football as a coach, I'm making official decisions every day. Whether he caught the ball, whether it was holding, he pushed off, he's run out of bounds, I see it full speed every day. They only see it full speed on Sunday, they're not anywhere near as good at officiating as I am. I officiate every day in practice. I've told them this many times; if they would come to practice, they'd work on Sunday travel Monday and Tuesday, they'd be here on Wednesday, Thursday, and Friday to officiate our practices. We'd welcome them, we'd entertain them, we'd do everything for them. But work full speed practices, Wednesday, Thursday, Friday. Travel on Friday night, and get in on Saturday, work the game on Sunday, get two days off. Three days a week full speed, then they'd be better officials. They all can recite the rules, but it's hard. They make honest mistakes. I don't question their integrity; they just make honest mistakes because they don't see it full speed.

Your fans always noticed you on the sidelines without any expressions during the game. Why was that?

Those are personality traits. You look at most cases, you look at coaches and they walk the whole time. There's a practical side to that also in that I had a headset on and I didn't have a long cord. I had a button on my side that I had to push three switches with. I'm talking to the offensive people, the defensive people, and the kicking game people. So when we're on defense, I want to know what we do on third and short that we didn't do the last time we didn't stop them. I'm talking constantly to people upstairs. Or somebody got hurt on the kickoff team, who the replacement is going to be. "No, I don't want that guy, I want the other guy," you know, that kind of thing. I'm constantly going over offense, defense, I know every play that's called before it's called, and you know, I've been around long enough, I don't really overrule the coaches very often, but I do if I think I want this guy out, I want this guy in, I want this play called on third and short next time, what's the play action, what is the goal line plays, you know, we're on the eighteen yard line, we're going in, what do we got inside the five, does that look as good as we had it before the game? Those are things I'm going through all the time. I don't have time to do all the other stuff. To be walking or back slapping or talking or jawing at the officials. It's all business. We spend two-and-a-half hours, sixteen times a year—that's our job to prepare for that. And that's why I have the headsets on without expression—I'm talking to everybody.

How did your family play into your schedule during the season?

Somebody said once, "What do you need to be a successful head coach?" Well, I said the first thing you've got to have is a patient wife. Then you have to have a loyal dog. You've got to have somebody you can holler at. Then you have to have a great quarterback. The patient wife is the main thing. She's in charge of the family, her decisions and all the things having a family is . . . that's vitally important. It takes the burden off of me. If the bicycle doesn't work, it's not that my wife doesn't fix the bicycle, but she can make sure somebody's going to fix the bicycle. And she'll do that. That's the family side of it and, if you notice the coaches I hired, all had families. They all had basically more than one child. So we all had the same problems, that's . . . what I'm trying to say is we all had the same advantages, we had to make time for our families, they took precedence and I think that makes you a more well-rounded person to go through the rigors of a coaching season and a career of coaching because we had a stable family operation

JERRY BURNS

HEAD COACH 1986-1991

Photo taken 1977

STATS

HIGH SCHOOL

Name of School: Detroit, Michigan Catholic
    Central High
Location of School: Detroit, Michigan
Graduation Year: 1944
Position: Quarterback
Number: 10
Height: 5 feet 10 inches
Weight: 160 pounds
Coach: Bob Wines
Other sports played: Baseball, basketball

COLLEGE

Name of School: University of Michigan
Location of School: Ann Arbor, Michigan
Graduation Year: 1951
How long attended: Four years
Did you graduate? Yes. February 1951.
Degree: Physical Education
Position: Quarterback
Number: 25
Height: 5 feet 10 inches
Weight: 160 pounds
Coach: Ben Osterbann
Other sports played: None

Where and why did you start coaching?

I guess I always wanted to get into coaching. I played in high school and in college and I was just a very average player, but I always liked all aspects of athletics. I came out of Michigan in 1951. My only claim to fame is that I played in the last minute of the Rose Bowl with Michigan. We played California in 1951. We beat them 14-6, but anyway . . .

My first coaching job was at the University of Hawaii—I go by football years—so that would have been football year 1951. I coached with George Allen at Whittier College for a couple years. I was back at a big catholic high school in Detroit and from there I went to Iowa and I was at Iowa for twelve years. Five years I was there as head coach. I finished there after the 1965 season and I was up with the Green Bay Packers with Vince Lombardi for the first two Super Bowls and came over to the Minnesota Vikings, back in football years again, in 1968. I was with the Vikings from 1968-91. I was with them twenty-three years. I worked with them on a part-time situation with Bud Grant up in Winnipeg in the summer. He used to bring in advisory coaches from the colleges and universities in the states. I was with Iowa at the time and we were running a wing-T. Bud had just gotten the head coaching job at Winnipeg and he wanted me to come up and so I did, and put the wing-T in there up at Winnipeg. He had a quarterback by the name of Kenny Ploen who was a great player for us out of the University of Iowa and that pretty much tells you what my coaching career was. The last six years I was the head coach at the Minnesota Vikings.

When you were at Iowa, you had some great players on your team who went on to the Vikings, right?

Yeah, we did. Wally Hilgenberg was one of them. I'm just trying to think . . . Paul Krause who I recruited out of Bendle High

School. Paul was signed already with the Washington Redskins. He spent two years with the Redskins. Actually when I came over here, Jim Finks, who was the general manager at the time, asked me about Paul Krause. I said he's as good a defensive back as I've seen and I just came from the Green Bay Packers where we had Willy Wood and Herb Adderley—two guys in the Hall of Fame. [Bob] Jeter at right cornerback who played for me at Iowa and Paul Krause were ranked with those guys. We had a kid by the name of Mike Riley, a linebacker who played about three to four years with the Bears. I don't like to miss anybody, but your memory fades after coaching for years.

Did Fred Zambreletti or Frank Gilliam play for you?

Frank Gilliam played for me when I was coaching at Iowa. And actually, Frankie went with Bud Grant up to Winnipeg. Actually, Frankie did not play for the Minnesota Vikings, but then Jerry Reichow was an Iowa guy. Then Jerry Reichow went with Jim Finks in the personnel department. I'm talking about football personnel—scouting and whatnot. Frankie Gilliam was at the University of Iowa coaching for a period of time and also played for us. Frankie also played on the 1956 Rose Bowl team we had. I'm just trying to think if we had other guys who went on to play in professional football—both in Canada and the National Football League. But those are the only guys who associated with Iowa who went with the Minnesota Vikings.

What position you were coaching with Vince Lombardi in Green Bay?

I was a defensive back coach. I was very fortunate when I came in. As I pointed out earlier, at left corner we had Herb Adderley from Michigan State who went on to the Hall of Fame, and at the right cornerback we had Bob Jeter from Iowa, Willie Wood from Southern California, who was also in the Hall of Fame. We had a guy named Tom Brown from Maryland who was a strong safety. Phil Bengtson was the head defensive coach at the Packers at the time and ended up succeeding Vince Lombardi at Green Bay. We had a guy named Hog [Dave] Hanner who was our defensive line coach. I'll say this unequivocally, as far as all of the football that I was concerned with, Phil Bengtson was the finest defensive coach that I've ever known.

Vince Lombardi was legendary and his namesake is the trophy that every team dreams of winning. What was his secret to becoming such an incredible leader?

First of all, everything you've heard about Vince Lombardi is true. I'm sure you've always heard good things and Lombardi was a tough guy. He was a tough guy to work with, but very, very fair. He was a very smart man. He handled the offense, and, as I pointed out, Phil Bengtson handled the defense. He had great player control, much like Bud Grant had. Lombardi was a tremendously intelligent guy. He coached under Red Blake for the Army. He was a very religious guy who daily went to mass for communion; he was a Roman Catholic. Lombardi was, as I pointed out, a hard person to work for but he was very fair. I can tell you one quick story. After the first Super Bowl, we played Kansas City and we won the game. We were flying back after the Super Bowl and, through some malfunction of the plane, we were grounded and we stayed at a big hotel right out by the airport there in Los Angeles—that would have been in 1966. Anyway, we had a big party and Lombardi was really happy and he went around and greeted all the wives with a big hug and everything was great. We got back to Green Bay at about 4:00 on Monday afternoon and he got all the coaches together and said, "You guys really did a great job. Take tomorrow off. We'll meet Wednesday at 8:00 in the morning!"

We got a day off and we had to come back the next day and break down the film and look at prospects we're gonna draft and everything like that. I think his secret was that he was always the first guy in the office and the last one to leave. He was a tough guy to work for as I said, but a very fair guy.

Do you have a Super Bowl ring from Super Bowl I?

Yeah. I got a Super Bowl ring from Super Bowl I, I got a Super Bowl ring from Super Bowl II, and I have four second place Super Bowl rings from the Minnesota Vikings.

How did you become a Minnesota Vikings coach?

I pointed out earlier that I worked for Bud for five years up in Winnipeg as an advisory coach. A funny thing happened. I was at Green Bay after the 1966 season. I had been out scouting and I landed in Green Bay and in the car on the way home it came over the radio that Bud Grant had just been named head coach of the Minnesota Vikings. That was in 1966. I walked in the house and I told my wife, Maryln, "You know, Maryln, I just heard on the radio that Bud Grant's head coach of the Minnesota Vikings." I had hardly said this when the phone rang, and it was Bud Grant. He said, "Jerry, how would you like to come over and be my offensive coordinator?" I thought about it and I said, "Bud, I've only been with Lombardi up in Green Bay for one year. I don't think I really paid my dues helping these guys as much as I hoped that I could or would. I think I'm going to stay here for the '67 season." After the '67 season with Green Bay again, we won the Super Bowl, Lombardi retired. Phil Bengtson was hired and Phil wanted me to stay as a defensive backfield coach and Bud called me again and said, "I've held the job open. I'd like to have you come over as our offensive coordinator." I thought about it, and said, "Well, I've seen the change here and when things like that change, you have a downward trend when you have a coach as great as Lombardi and replaced by Phil Bengtson—I don't in any way mean to demote Phil Bengtson, in my opinion, he's a great coach. I really always liked offensive coaching and I decided to take Bud up on his offer and come over here as the offensive coordinator. I was the offensive coordinator for twenty-three years, I was here for seventeen years, and the other six years, I was head coach.

You came to the Vikings in 1968 as the offensive coordinator and the Vikings went to the first Super Bowl in 1969. Did you use any of your concepts over the years or did you have a system down before you came to the Vikings?

It's pretty much the same, pretty much repetitious, just some little changes, and nomenclature changes. One team counts the right shots and to the left of the center is weak, and one team would call an off-tackle play a one-thirty-two and the other would call a one-forty-two or something. When I came in I put almost the same offensive that we were running at Iowa and patterned it after the wing-T and in professional aspects of the game, I would say that the first year we were successful enough that we played. In those days with Joe Kapp as a quarterback, we played with what they call a second place play-off and we were beat by Baltimore. The next year we did win the championship game and we played Kansas City with Hank Stram—it's too bad about Hank passing away—but we played Hank Stram in the Super Bowl after the 1968 season.

In 1971, you went back to the Super Bowl. How was the team the first year with Joe Kapp compared with Fran Tarkenton as a quarterback?

We were a good team. Both teams were very good. The 1968 team with Joe Kapp was a physically more imposing type of team patterned after Joe Kapp's mannerisms, but the 1971 team was a very good team as well. You know, you don't get to the Super Bowl if you don't have a pretty good team. I would say that overall, the 1971 team was probably better than the 1968 team with the exception of the mannerisms that surrounded the 1968 team were more rough and tumble, a street fight gang of guys like Lonnie Warwick, Joe Kapp, of course, and Billy Brown and all the guys we had in that ball club. We got a little more refinement to the 1971 team with Fran Tarkenton as we moved a little bit more and more to the passing game. Then the team really started to blossom when we got Chuck Foreman. A lot of Chuck Foreman's success has to be attributed to guys like Dave Osborn and Bill Brown because they showed Chuck the ropes and how hard you had to play, how hard you had to practice, and how hard you had to prepare. So you can't say enough about any of the teams without including guys like Dave Osborn and Billy Brown.

So to make a team successful, you need players more than the plays?

I'm looking at one right now who was a hell of a player, Matt Blair. You know the saying "To Hell with the plays, give me the players!" I mean you've got to have the players, obviously, you gotta have good player control, you gotta have a basic sound system offensively and defensively, and you've got to have players not necessarily who have great ability from a football standpoint, but who have great ability to work together and to work hard and to ensure that the rest of the players are practicing hard and playing hard and preparing hard for the game. Certainly a big part of it is the coach's responsibility to prepare the team for a game, but just as much a part of success is that the players have to prepare themselves.

Fran Tarkenton was a great scrambler. Was he a great athlete?

There's no question about it. Fran was a great athlete. They keep talking about little Fran Tarkenton. I would say Fran was probably 6 feet 1 inch, about 205 pounds, but he was put together as well as any quarterback as I've seen play in the National Football League. He was a very, very smart guy and a very competitive guy. He had great leadership qualities about him. Everything about Tarkenton was first class. He's a Hall of Famer. No question, everyone thinks all he was, was a scrambler. Yes, he could scramble, he could run, he could throw that ball, and his percentages in throwing were excellent coupled with his completions and the total number of passes that he was involved in. So everything that you say about Fran Tarkenton has got to be a plus.

You've also coached Tommy Kramer. Between him and Fran Tarkenton, which quarterback would you use inside the red zone?

When you talk about red zone, I've always said that the way I analyze or evaluate a quarterback is by what he does inside the ten-yard line. Does he want to control the offense at that point? Some quarterbacks would just as soon run a draw play or run a sweep or run some kind of a trap. Tarkenton—and I'll say the same thing about Tommy Kramer—they wanted a ball in their hands and the only thing they asked out of me is whether I wanted a roll out or a bootleg. Somebody, some receiver in the flat, they wanted a trail-in receiver or maybe a late-break receiver. Both those guys would say, "Coach, don't worry about me getting sacked with the ball or fumbling that ball. I'll either throw the pass or complete it or I'll run the ball or if I'm getting trapped, I'll throw the ball away." And those guys had all the confidence in their own ability and they wanted to shoulder the responsibility.

With the running backs, you had some good ones in Bill Brown, Dave Osborn, Chuck Foreman, Darrin Nelson, Herschel Walker, and Rickey Young. Each one played a big role for you, but which one stood out for you?

I don't think there's any question that Chuck Foreman was all around one of the great backs who played in the National Football League. He's a great receiver, coming out of the backfield. You know when he was at Miami, they always sent him out as a planker to catch the ball. His running ability, great balance, lateral moves and more than adequate speed—everything about Chuck Foreman was pretty much a plus.

Bill Brown. When I was at Green Bay, the guy that they feared the most, from any other guy in the National Football League at that time was Bill Brown. I'll say this about Bill Brown—and if Rickey Young says this isn't the truth it's because Rickey Young was a hell of a blocker—but Bill Brown was probably the best blocking back that I've seen or coached in the National Football League. Rickey Young was damn good too. But Bill Brown was a great receiver. Bill Brown had great balance and great power. Bill Brown was a great team player and everything about Bill Brown was first class. He was a great one.

Herschel Walker was a great player. I mean an underlying great. I think Herschel got saddled with the responsibility that would give him a comparative position that was given for him in a trade. I'm not being critical of Mike Lynn. Mike Lynn was very fair with me, but I think the trade was way overbalanced. In addition, we lost six players who were returning because of the draft choice they were involved in. Herschel Walker was one of the most charismatic guys I have ever been around. I'd say on at least four or five occasions he's come to me and say, "Hey, Coach, I'll cover kick-offs for you, I'll cover punts for you, I'll run back kick-offs, anything to help this ball club." He was one of the first guys to be at a meeting. He was one of the first guys on the field. He'd do everything. Everything about Herschel Walker is "A-plus." But again, the trade wasn't an even balance. He did a great job for us.

What are your thoughts about Rickey Young and Chuck Foreman in the back field together, and how they once called a play on the goal line where Rickey switched position and let Chuck run the ball?

We used to call that the red zone. In fact, that was our red offense. The red offense meant that we always had in two tight ends and we had both our backs in and they were both Rickey Young and Chuck Foreman. We had what we call the Powerhouse and the Flanker and whatnot. We used to send the red offensive plays in and I sent in a play that was a Powerhouse right and we were going to run a 22 lead. They came out and I saw the two backs lined up wrong. I thought, "Gee, that guy must have given the wrong play," but they ran the 22 lead in for the touchdown, with Rickey Young blocking and Foreman carrying the ball. "What the hell's going on?" I said to them after the play. "I thought I sent in a Powerhouse? You guys line up, you saw what the hell's going on!" Ol' Rickey says, "Well Coach, I wanted to block for Foreman and let him carry the ball." He was one of the finest football players that ever played here: Rickey Young. And he's another guy who could catch the ball coming out of the backfield. He's another guy who could run. He's another guy who was a great blocker and a great team player. He and Bill Brown. I patterned those two guys after each other.

How did it come about that you were offered the head coaching job for the Vikings?

Well, you know, Bud retired after the 1984 season, and they brought in Les Steckel. Now I'm going to say this: I don't think Les was ready to be the head coach at the time. I think he had some ideas that were way out of line as far as conditioning and pre-season practice. He was a very sharp guy, but I think the team had a disaster. I think it was a 3-13 year, and he was fired.

Bud then came back to the 1985 season. At the time, I was on my way to go with Marty Schottenheimer to the Cleveland Browns and at the last minute Bud offered me an opportunity I really couldn't turn down: to stay as the offensive coordinator. I told Marty Schottenheimer that Bud was a really close friend of mine, and this was the decision I made, and he understood.

After the 1985 season, Bud retired. I was down in Jamaica with my family and got a call from Mike Lynn. "I want you to meet me," he said. He was staying at the Half Moon Resort in Jamaica. He was on one side of Montego Bay and I was on the other.

I said, "What the hell happened now? What did I do now?" What had happened was there was some problem with the owner, Max Winter. I thought, "What the hell am I involved in?" and so I went over there and said, "Yeah, Mike. What's happening?"

He looked at me and said, "I'm offering you the head coaching job at the Minnesota Vikings."

"What happened to Bud? Is there any kind of problem?" I asked.

"Bud resigned, and I'm offering you the head coaching job." That's how I got the job.

What was the team like your first year as head coach?

In 1986, my first coaching year, we had a pretty solid team. We had to bring a team back from a 3-13. We were 9-7, I think, our first year. That was probably the best all around team that we had when I was there. Tommy Kramer was playing great, Wade Wilson was doing a hell of a job. We had just gotten Rich Gannon and he was great. Actually, Rich may have come the next year . . . that was the strike year and Mike Lynn made the decision that we weren't going to go get any other players. Either way, we had a very, very, very good team. Because of the shortened season, any team with a 500 or better put them in the playoffs. We played New Orleans, who had a very good team. Jim Mora was the coach down there and we beat those guys. Tommy Kramer played, Wade Wilson did a great job. We then went out and played the 49ers. This was one of the few times we played the 49ers that we beat them on their field. [Steve] Young was their quarterback, and they had Jerry Rice and a great compliment of people.

I just want to say this about that game we played against the 49ers: it was one of the few times I've ever seen a wide receiver dominate a game. I don't know how many balls he caught, ten or twelve. He had the record at that time. I don't know if they've beaten that record or not but Anthony Carter was a great player, a great receiver. He could run with the ball after a great catch. He was a great competitor, everything about him. Wade Wilson would just go back there and throw an "H" pattern, throw an out pattern, throw a fly pattern, a break in pattern, whatever you need. He'd throw it up there and Anthony Carter went and got it. He actually completely dominated. I mean I've seen running backs, quarterback, and linebackers dominate games, but I've never seen a wide receiver do it. Even so, we beat those guys and then we played Washington in the championship game. And we got beat there but I think it was something like 17-7. That was probably the best team I had.

Have the players over the years who you've coached kept in touch with you?

You know, so many of the players don't live here. Everybody comes up to me over the years . . . I've lived here for thirty-eight years, and they say, "You still live here?" and I say "Yeah, I've been here all my life!" But the guys who are in town I still see. As a matter of fact, just this morning, Rickey Young was over at my house. He brought some balls over for a friend of his he wanted me to autograph. I still see Rickey Young, Bill Brown. I've bumped into Rich Gannon setting up a little golf game. I sometimes see Dave Osborn, I see Stu Voigt a lot, Mick Tingelhoff. The guys who are in town I see at various golf deals or Vikings deals or situations where we're bringing back the veterans when they've included me, so I still see them. Everybody's got favorite players. I tell you my two favorite players who I had were Stu Voigt and Rickey Young. They are both great guys, great competitors . . . those two guys . . . I just love those two guys.

One of the things that the players have said about you was that you could never remember their names. Why was that?

I don't know. I'll say that identified me for a long time. I'm a little excitable, you know. One day, some reporter asked Darrin Nelson about what Burnsie said on the TV. And he said, "I don't know. I can't understand him." They say I talk too fast or things of that consequence, but maybe my mouth works faster than my brain. I see some guy and I can't think of his name, and I say, "Hey, you. Come here, I want to talk to you." I remember, he's a guy who's a great player and I said, "Hey number ten, hey ten! Grab number ten!" I see some guys and their names pop right in your mind and most of the times I call them . . . like Tingelhoff. I call him Ting. "Hey, Ting, you do this!" or I'd call Irwin, Irv. "Hey, Irv!" But some guys, like Rickey Young, it's "Rickey this" or "Rickey that." I guess I don't know why. I can't answer that. I've been, I don't want to say criticized, but it's been pointed out that I can't remember names and all I can say is they are all friends of mine and if I've ever hurt anybody, I apologize, but I know the guys. I know he's a football player and he's a friend of mine. I know him but I can't think of his name.

There were always a lot of pranks going on, especially at training camp. The players always liked to try and scare you. What were some of the scariest, funniest, or stupidest pranks played on you?

One time Clinton Jones, the halfback from Michigan State—I loved that guy too. I think at the time he was rooming with Gene Washington, who was also from Michigan State. Anyway, I knocked on the door and they always answered with, "Who's there?" in a growl.

"It's the coach," I'd say.

"Open the door."

So I open the door and he's got these snakes around his neck! It scared the hell out of me! "What the hell!" I'd say.

"They're my pets."

All I could say was, "Do they come when you call?"

One time in a team meeting with the offense, we were show- ing some film and I looked up on the screen and there was this big bug on the screen. It kept going back and forth, but I couldn't slap it away. Finally I turn off the projector and I say, "What the hell is going on here? Turn the lights on!" And these guys, Tarkenton and Bill Brown and Tingelhoff and some other guys, they had a big black bug that they had somehow strung across the ceiling and was dropping it right in front of my face and I was scared to death! But anyhow, they were fun guys and it was all in good fun. But I'll tell you, I don't like snakes, and I don't like bugs!

Your wife has an interesting spelling of her name. She spells is without an "i".

That's right. It's spelled M-A-R-Y-L-N. There is no "i". So anytime she writes her name down, someone says it's Marilyn. If someone calls up our house and they ask for Marilyn, I always say, "You've got the wrong number." Recently, Maryln has had a very severe back operation. She's getting better, but it'll be some time before she's completely up and about, but she's doing fine. So now it's my turn to take care of her. We have five kids, and my son, Michael, was a ball boy for the Vikings. We have four daughters. We have fifteen grandkids of which we've got eight boys and seven girls, so I'm ahead of the ledger in that regard anyway.

Can you name them all, or do you say "Hey number 10, get over here!"

I say, "Hey you . . . !" or "Hey, brother, get this or get that for Grandpa!" But my family has been very wonderful to me with recognizing some of the problems that you go through in coaching and living their life with me.

Do the coaches get retirement benefits? And if so, how many years do they have to put in?

Yeah, the [coaches'] retirement package with the NFL is entirely different than the players' retirement. Actually, you get complete retirement after fifteen years.

I think after a certain amount of years, you're entitled to a certain amount of money, but I'm not exactly sure on that. But there is a retirement for NFL coaches, and it has no relationship at all with the retirement plan that's involved with the players.

What advice do you have for the kids who want to become professional football players?

You could write a book on a question like that. The one thing that scares me more than any one thing nowadays about kids is the drugs. To fool around with or be associated with any of the drug culture is the worst thing that can happen to any kid. Particularly with anybody who's interested in athletics, but certainly to anybody. I would also say that just as important is their education. They've got to get their education. Apply themselves at school, whether that be in high school or college or whatever they do. They've got to get a solid education. They've got to recognize the need for discipline. I see kids out there shooting baskets or playing football and all they're really thinking about is the NBA or

NFL. This is fine. It's great to have that dream, but they've got to go through the action of disciplining themselves with the educational facets that surround athletics, whether that be basketball, football, baseball, or whatever that might be. You can take one hundred guys out shooting baskets and maybe one guy makes the NBA, and you don't want the other ninety-nine guys to be fooling around with the street gangs or drugs or anything of that question.

MIKE TICE

HEAD COACH   2001-PRESENT

Photo taken 2005

HIGH SCHOOL
Name of School: Central Islip High Sch
Location of School: Central Islip, New Y
Graduation Year: 1977
Position: Quarterback
Jersey number: 14
Height: 6 feet 7 inches
Weight: 222 pounds
40 speed: 4.75 seconds
Coach: George O'Leary
Other sports played: Basketball

COLLEGE
Name of School: Maryland
Location of School: College Park, Maryland
How long attended: 4 years
Did you graduate? No
Position: Quarterback
Jersey number: 14
Height: 6 feet 7 inches
Weight: 235 pounds
40 speed: 4.75 seconds
Coach: Jerry Claiborne
Other sports played: None

PRO
Position: Tight End
Jersey number: 86/87
Free Agent/Other: 1981, free agent
Year Retired: 1995
Height: 6 feet 8 inches
Weight: 262 pounds
40 speed: 5.0 seconds
Coach: Jack Patera

Is there an advantage for you being a player and then becoming a coach?

Yeah, I think a couple things. Initially, it gives you some respect from the players because they know you've done it. It doesn't guarantee that the respect carries on; you have to earn that respect over time. But as far as knowing the mentality of the players, what day of the week their bodies hurt, when you can push them, and what type of mood they're in, I think it helps with all those different situations.

How do owners make a difference in your schedule of day-to-day activities, or do they affect you at all?

Well, as a head coach, dealing with Mr. McCombs, it's basically done with phone calls a couple days a week just to bring him up to speed on decisions made throughout the course of the week and to get any thoughts that he might have on some issues pertaining to the club. As far as scheduling, I set the schedule, set what we are trying to accomplish during the day, during the week, and we just stay to that.

What is your greatest loss that has affected you the most over the years and what is your greatest win that has given you the most inspiration?

Well, the toughest defeat, there have been two of them. Both have been recent. One was a defeat as an assistant coach in Atlanta in the championship game to go to the Super Bowl, here at the Metrodome. The other was here at the last second loss in Arizona the last play of the game to clinch the division. Both of those losses were significant. Both of those losses hurt very, very, very much. The biggest win that I can remember was actually as a player. It was on New Year's Eve down in Miami. We were not even supposed to be in the game, and we beat Miami. Double-digit underdogs, we

---

MIKE TICE   **197**

beat Miami late in the game to go to the AFC Championship Game the next week against the L.A. Raiders in the Coliseum. That was the most fun, the biggest win, the most significant win. The next biggest win as a coach was the playoff victory against Green Bay this particular season.

Do you take time, or do you find time to get in a workout program?

You know, my body is not as good as it used to be and during the season I was very dedicated to getting four walks in a week—two miles plus a walk, and two lifts in. And I'm very dedicated to it. Since the season has ended, I haven't worked out yet! It's been tough. I've been in and out of town a lot, and I haven't gotten the chance to even take a walk since the season ended. As the off-season progresses, as we get closer to mini-camp, I'll start back into training again—if you can call that training—but at my age when you've been beat up a little bit, and getting ready on April 26th to have ankle surgery, it's harder and harder to jog, or certainly to sprint.

As a head coach, you have to make all the schedule changes and an outline of what goes on throughout the weekday. Can you walk us through the whole week on a schedule program?

During the in-season, it's pretty well lined out. Let's start with Monday. Monday, the day after the game, the first thing you want to do is look at the film before you go to a staff meeting at 11:00 and sit down with the coaches. You let them know how you see the game, and get the feedback from them how they see the game. At some point in the morning, you go down and visit with the trainers staff, and see how the injuries are mounting up, see what things you have to tell the coaches about concerns, injuries about players who might not be available that next week, etc.

Then the hardest part of the week is dealing with the media Monday; you have the press conference, certainly after a loss, it's tough, it's demanding, and it's usually about 1:00. Then the players will come in. We'll meet with the players and talk about the game; they'll break off with their assistants and look at the game. I'll come back up and we'll continue to either finish the film or, if I have finished it, we'll move on to the next game. And so Monday's pretty well set that way and once everything's done, it's already 4:00 and you just move along with the next game.

What I like to try and do is watch enough of the film by late Monday night so I can come in Tuesday and give the coaches my thoughts on how to approach the game. You know, discuss the weaknesses of our football team that they might exploit and then just the opposite the other way. I usually have some media interviews that day, but it's not particularly too bad. We'll have a staff meeting in the afternoon on Tuesday and get the initial game plan from the coaches. Then at night, we have a catered family dinner where the coaches come and bring their kids—we have a lot of young kids.

Wednesday's a workday: get up in the morning, have a staff meeting before we do anything, talk about the day, update the coaches on the injuries, and then we go down and have a team meeting. We'll talk to the team about the schedule for the week, you know, how we are going to approach the game, and then it's a regular practice day from there. We have a walk through at 11:15, we go out for practice at 2:00, and that's really a pretty easy day as far as scheduling because it's laid out for the whole season the same way. Wednesday night we continue to look at practice film, then I have a radio show Wednesday night that cuts into my day significantly. It's a two-and-a-half-hour ordeal—driving and coming back—basically it's a pain in the neck is what it is. Then I come back and try to catch up with the coaches on how they saw practice.

Thursday, same type of deal. Get up in the morning, have a staff meeting. Go over injuries with the coaches and see the game plan: talk about things we didn't like, things to throw out or fix. Then we have a team meeting where I talk to the team again briefly, walk through practice, etc. Thursday's a nice day because Monday night I'm probably not out of here until 1:00-1:30 AM, Tuesday night probably not out of here until 12:30 AM, Wednesday night I'm probably not out of here until about midnight. But Thursday's nice, because I'll watch the practice film and I'm gone, so I might be home at 6:00 PM.

Friday's nice also—it's a short day for everybody. We have a staff meeting first, then a team meeting, then a brief walk through in practice schedule. We then have lunch in the locker room which is nice, and most of us are out of here about 2:30 on Friday which is also nice. On Fridays, I get a little family time.

On Saturdays, I come in whether it's a travel day or not. On travel days, I come in and have a staff meeting. I like to meet every day with the staff, but I don't meet with the team Saturday morning because I have my big meeting with the team Saturday night. They have their briefing; we go over our last reviews, special teams call up, etc. And then, if we're at home, I'm on the couch watching college football. If we're away, I'll go home, get changed, and get to the airport. I always drive to the airport. If we're in a hotel, I'll have the coaches in my room. We'll have some appetizers, stuff like that, and do a team meeting. I don't like to leave the hotel and go out to dinner often when we're away. I do it occasionally. After I have a team meeting, I'll go back to my room and watch television. And that's really what I do.

I'm up early on Sundays, and I can't really eat. I eat very light on game day; my stomach's going on game day, the same as a player. I'll have a little fruit, something, banana, coffee, and then head down the stadium. One last thing, I forgot. I'm Catholic, so on Saturday nights we have a Catholic mass fifteen minutes after the team meeting. So that's a week during the season.

The off-season's a little bit different. I don't like to meet in the early morning with the coaches when we don't have something going on like development-camp or mini-camp, so our staff meeting is normally at 9:00 AM. That's about what time I get in. We have ongoing meetings throughout the course of the day, sometimes with the personnel staff. Scott Studwell sometimes, [Paul] Wiggins, he's the pro personnel. We always meet with the coaches in the morning. If it's a development-camp or min-camp, we're working on a draft. I'm like any other worker in the off-season,

I'm done at 4:00 or 4:30 PM. If there's something going on, a free-agent in town, I might carry on 5:00 PM, something like that. I try to keep it in a normal working day during the off-season because during the on-season, it's an eighty-hour week.

As a head coach, when things go wrong, who do you turn to?

Well, you know, it's tough. My dad passed in '87, so I don't really have anyone that I can lean on as far as an elder. Occasionally when things aren't going right, I might call Red [McCombs] and run something by him. I like to go down and talk to Coach Grant once in awhile when things aren't going well. I'm fortunate to have him in the building. I go down to Coach Wiggins once in awhile because he has an office in our building and runs our pro personnel department. And once in awhile I pick up the phone and call Coach O'Leary. George O'Leary. So those are the kind of guys I turn to when things aren't going right.

When you're coaching, you have to have a balance with your family. What does your work take away from your family because of your busy schedule during the season?

Well, my kids are both actively involved with sports, and I make an attempt to attend every single sporting event if time allows—and you can make time, if you are dedicated to your family. Soccer matches—I don't like soccer. Track meets—I love track. There are also basketball games and football games. My wife, Dianne, attends every single game and so that's a good family bonding thing. We try to have dinner together as much as we can, although it's hard during the season. Eating meals together as a family is a lost art and it's also the time when you communicate as a family, so we try to do that as much as we can.

We always take our spring breaks together, although now that my daughter's a senior in high school, there's been some talk of her trying to, you know, go in another direction, but as long as they're under my roof, we take spring break together. When they were younger it was a little easier to say, "Friday night, let's go to Mall of America as a family," and we'd all go down there and eat and walk around the mall. We used to like to go to Canterbury Downs. They have live bands there and the kids would hang out on the infield and listen to music, my wife and I would sit on the picnic table, and I might smoke a cigar. Those are good family bonding times. Certainly when we are in town, we try to go to St. Patrick's Church together. It's hard to do things as a family, but you try. I think it starts with us being an athletic family. We try to be involved in all the athletic events that we can.

You were throwing the red flag a little bit too often during your first couple years. Do you have anything to talk about or elaborate on that?

Well, you know, I heard that comment from people but then when you look at the study of the league, I'm right at the league average, so there's been some comments made I threw the flag too much but then there were never any statistics to back it up, so I actually disagree. We have put in a format that I followed this year that, except for once, against the Giants, the coaches in the booth control decided whether the flag should be thrown or not unless I'm 100 percent sure—like I did in New Orleans, when I won two challenges. As far the comments about throwing too much, I think that people making those comments haven't looked at any stats.

Special Olympics has been something close to your heart. Is this one of your favorite charities to work with?

The Special Olympics has always been dear to me. I was on the Board of the Special Olympics in Washington State and Alaska when I was a player for the Seahawks. I was asked by Brad Madson to get back involved with Special Olympics when I became a head coach. It's a lot harder, as you know, to be involved with charities as an assistant coach. As a head coach, you can make some time and there are some windows on Tuesday because you are not spending the whole day on game planning. I think Special Olympics is key for me because it's genuine. What you get is a real emotion from the athletes. I'm certainly involved heavily in youth sports. I have coached youth sports, baseball, basketball, and football extensively for a number of years, and am now heavily involved in youth clinics—football clinics for youth. There was one I was working on this morning that will take place at St. Thomas this summer in conjunction with John and my football camp. We have one big one playing in Mankato, so that is something I am heavily involved in. But any type of thing to deal with children I think is very critical to be involved in.

If you had anything to add or say to young people in sports, to look at their future, what would you share with them?
Well, I would say this: there are so much politics in youth sports nowadays and there are a lot of decisions that are made for the kids—play time, positions—before they even have a chance to compete. I think that kids should set goals for themselves and that they should work to achieve those goals and don't let anybody tell them that they can't achieve those goals and don't let anybody frustrate you. Just keep working, and if you just keep working and keep playing, and well, the cream always rises to the top. At some point you'll be able to play for a good coach who is going to realize that you have talent. Now, unfortunately for the youth of our nation, you don't play for a good coach half the time. But if you continue to not get depressed and not get discouraged and fight the fight, I think you'll succeed if you stick to it.

PERSONNEL AND MEDIA

FRED ZAMBRELETTI

HEAD TRAINER

Photo taken 2005

*Interview taped at Winter Park, Eden Prairie, Minnesota,
March 2005*

What is your favorite story from the first year the Vikings became a professional franchise team?

It's 1961. We're going to our first training camp in Bemidji, Minnesota. The whole state was excited to have pro football in Minnesota. Back then, Bemidji was a resort city, so there were a lot of people who came to watch us practice. Our first coach was Norm Van Brocklin, who was a very demanding individual. The Vikings were involved in public relations throughout the state, and we had a camp for a lot of young guys from around the state.

Anybody who wanted to tryout got to tryout. We had a number of people from all the small colleges in the state: Winona, Duluth, Superior, Bemidji, St. Cloud, St. Thomas, St. John's—we had somebody from everywhere.

We had one guy who showed up who wanted to try out. He was a squatty little guy—a bartender from Detroit and he had a great big beer belly to prove it. Of course we wouldn't pass him on the physical and when he asked why, I said jokingly, "We were scared that somebody'd hit that big belly and give you a double hernia!"

He takes a step closer to me, looks me in the eyes with this mean look, and says, "Believe me. There are a lot of guys that have already hit this belly!"

Training camp at that time was about eight or nine weeks long, and the first practice was going to be picture day on a Sunday morning with all these young guys. Well, the people in the news media were reluctant to go all the way to Bemidji when it was just picture day with the recruits and they knew we'd have another picture day in a week with all the players. So when [Norm] Van Brocklin saw nobody came, he said, "Well, no use wasting the day," and we went into a full practice.

We had those young guys practice hard that day and that night, you could hear those same tough young guys going out the doors and even through the windows with their suitcases as they jumped ship. Eight guys left that first night. I heard one guy say as he was leaving, "If this is what picture day is like, there's no way I'm going to be here for practice!"

What high school did you go to and what year did you graduate?
Melcher Public high in Melcher, Iowa. I graduated in 1950.

What sports did you play?
In high school? Football, basketball, baseball, but I went to a school where everybody played.

How big were you?

I was probably about six feet tall and about 190 pounds.

What position did you play in football?

I was a lineman, both offense and defense. You went both ways in those days.

What was your 40 speed in those days?

They timed me with an alarm clock!

Where did you go to college?

I went to the University of Iowa. I graduated in 1955, with a BA and then I went to graduate school for physical therapy at the University of Iowa as well. I stayed in Iowa to train, and then went to Hibbing, Minnesota, as chief therapist for the hospital and then from Hibbing I went to the University of Toledo as their trainer and then from there to the Vikings in 1961. I've been with the Vikings since the beginning.

What were the most common injuries you have seen through your career?

In the early days, I've probably had more foot injuries because the shoes weren't as good as they are today. We had the same injuries, pretty much that you have now, except in those days, you didn't have the surgical procedures to reconstruct the knee that you have so frequently today. And you didn't have the MRI to see a lot of these torn cartilages and everything. So if a guy had a serious injury back in those days, either he had the rest of his career to rehab from it, but if the ligaments were torn and were unstable, he either played with it or he retired.

What's the most serious injury that you worked on where you had to say "you can't play any more?"

Well, I told several of them that, but they didn't listen! Most were knee injuries.

Is the combine more important today for trainers to view the players before they're drafted?

Absolutely. You get a pretty good handle on seeing what's going on. If he's got degenerative arthritis in his knees, you know it then and can get a pretty good handle on it.

Is it harder to be drafted today through the medical side of it?

Well, so many players have had good reconstructions in college, and they've played with it. It's kind of like a process of natural selection. Those who get to this level have proven themselves that they can play with it. So you get that part of the history with them and you get to see how much time they missed and what injuries they had with it, so it's very important.

Who was the quickest healer?

There were many. You really can't list them all. Any of those guys who had those records that you read about, Jim [Marshall], Carl [Eller], Alan [Page], and all of them guys, they were all quick healers. They had to be quick healers to have the records that they had.

I had one ex-NFL coach who said, "Look. We have four defensive linemen here who must have played a total of sixty-four years or more of pro football, and missed four games." We got guys now who miss that much in a season. You know what I mean? And then I hear, "Yeah, but your guys didn't get medial collateral injuries, sprained ankles, and separated shoulders."

"Are you kidding me? What do you think we played, flag football? Of course we got those injuries. You couldn't stand it out there . . . "

Do you think the equipment is a lot better today?

The equipment's better, the shoes are better, the rules are better. In the earlier years they had those crack-back blocks, clothes-lines, and things of that nature and didn't try to police them as much. They like the speed, they like the contact, and they don't want anybody to get hurt, but how can you prevent it?

When a player gets hurt and he has to be on the mend, you have a program that's second to none to get them healthy again. What is that program?

Well, I've always felt that as a young trainer I received a good education in Iowa in the sciences as far as physiology and biology. I was never one to believe in a lot of machines. I believe God gave us a body that's far superior to any machines to heal us. I've always felt that if you could take a player and simply keep him active and keep him moving then take him up to a level of conditioning and yet not aggravate that area—keep that blood flowing through his system, then he would heal far greater than any machine could do. Plus the fact that when the athlete was focusing on sore muscles rather than his injured knee, all he could do was think about the return. The time of being on the mend was shortened for him, and he would be able to feel he was still a part of the team, because he was out there working instead of sitting around. With my experience growing up in a coal mining area and also my experience in the service, I always felt that we can do more than we think we can do. The mind will stop before the body and you can keep working, and I always like to have a player feel that he did something today that he didn't think he could do. I think that produced a lot of strong, tough people with the Minnesota Vikings. I've always felt that nobody gets hurt in conditioning. I'm right there with them, measuring their pulse, seeing what their heartbeat is. If we have a guy who has an ankle or a knee that is bothering him, don't ask him to cut on it, just go out and hit that belly every five yards. That takes a lot of muscles, and it accelerates, decelerates, and if he starts to hurt a little bit, he'll forget about that ankle.

In training camp, you once had somebody pushing the golf cart. Why?

That came from my physical therapy clinic in St. Paul. We were the second clinic in the United States to have a Cybex machine. Everybody thought this machine was going to cure all the knee problems, but it could also, if you weren't careful, aggravate a joint. But for the players who couldn't come to the clinic, I got this idea from one of the doctors from the Buffalo Bills when OJ Simpson injured his knee. OJ was traveling all over the country, and couldn't go to a therapy office. So this doctor had him do lateral step-ups. And that gave me an idea. Now, my clinic in St. Paul was on the 9th floor, and we'd have our patients walk up the stairs on the way to therapy, and we had a number of patients, and that stairway would be full. They're called "closed-chain exercises." Essentially, they are a functional activity with the leg, but the foot is on the ground. Because when the foot's on the ground, you have to use the hamstrings to stabilize the knee and by doing that we were putting Cybex companies out of business. So then we took this closed-chain exercise routine with us to camp and with no stairs or a Cybex machine, we had the players push the golf cart.

How do you feel about the four Super Bowl losses?

The older I get, the less significance I place on that. I remember the first Super Bowl against Kansas City and I cried like a baby. But I see more important things like the relationships and knowing the players so well and seeing their kids and their families. I think it's more important to know and to see what people have done, and to appreciate their characters.

Is there any advice you have for kids coming into the sporting world?

I think that the most important thing is to realize that although it's nice to have heroes, they are human. They should also think of sports as fun and to think that the value of the sport is to be a part of a team. At the same time, know that there are far greater things in this world than sports.

CHUCK BARTA

HEAD ATHLETIC TRAINER

Photo taken 2004

STATS

HIGH SCHOOL

Name of School: Columbia Heights High
School
Location of School: Columbia Heights,
Minnesota
Graduation Year: 1984
Other sports: Basketball

COLLEGE

Name of School: University of Wisconsin,
La Crosse
Location of School: La Crosse, Wisconsin
Graduation Year: 1988
How long attended: 4 years
Did you graduate? Yes
Degree: B.S. in Athletic Training

PRO

Current Position: Head Athletic Trainer
Years as Assistant Athletic Trainer: 1988-1998
Years as Head Trainer: 1999—Present

What is the first school you attended, and did you do any training at that time?

The University of Wisconsin, La Crosse, and the athletic training was mostly clinical hours, field hours for school.

At what point did you make the decision to be a trainer?

Well, in high school I injured my knee and consequently became interested in the medicine aspect of the sport. To become an athletic trainer, you have to go to a four-year college and the school I chose started you out in the program in my freshman year.

What's the first thing you need to do when a player comes in hurt?

You analyze the injury. When the player is injured, you have to calm them down and assess the treatment based on the injury. Whether that is ice, stretching, surgery, etc.

Did you specialize in football, baseball, or basketball?

They give you an all-around program. I worked basketball, softball, and wrestling. I did not work the varsity football; I worked the JV football and track. I had quite a few different sports I worked. You're not in the athletic training program until the second year, and you have to be picked as the top twenty of the class.

What years were you at Wisconsin?

I was there from 1984-88.

Did any of the players on your team make the pros?

Not from La Crosse, not when I was there. There were some athletes who made it prior to my being there and since I've been there.

How did you get into the pros after college?

I worked as an intern there my entire time and started here with the Vikings as an intern in 1985. I worked summer camps in 1985, '86, '87, '88 and went fulltime in 1988.

FRANK GILLIAM

DIRECTOR OF PLAYER PERSONNEL

Photo taken 2005

S T A T S

HIGH SCHOOL
Name of School: Stubenville High School
Location of School: Stubenville, Ohio
Graduation Year: 1952
Position: Offensive and Defensive End
Jersey number: 21
Height: 6 feet 2 inches
Weight: 165 pounds
40 speed: 4.75 seconds
Coach: Ray Hoyman
Other sports played: Basketball, baseball

COLLEGE
Name of School: University of Iowa
Location of School: Iowa City, Iowa
Graduation Year: January 1957
How long attended: 5 years
Did you graduate? Yes
Degree: BA in Physical Education
Position: Offensive and Defensive End
Jersey number: 87
Height: 6 feet 2 inches
Weight: 181-185 pounds
40 speed: 4.65-4.7 seconds
Coach: Forest Evashefski
Other sports played: None

PRO
Position: Offensive Receiver
Jersey number: 74
Year Drafted: 1957
Draft Round: Seventh–Green Bay
Year Retired: Released from Vancouver 1962
Height: 6 feet 2 inches
Weight: 197 pounds
40 speed: 4.65 seconds
Coach: Bud Grant (Winnipeg), Wayne Robinson, Dave Skrien (Vancouver)

What was your job after your retirement?

The first job I had was in Canada. I was a school teacher at a middle school, and I coached football at the Junior College level. Up there it was called Junior Football which was equivalent to American football at the Junior College. And then I taught soccer, softball, basketball at the middle school.

How many years did you play?

All total it was three years in Winnipeg and two years in Vancouver.

Could you share with us, your highest and your lowest salary for one year?

The highest probably was $8,500 and the lowest was like $7,000.

What is your title now with the Minnesota Vikings?

Senior consultant, player personnel.

Over the years, you've had opportunity to be a scout for the Vikings. How long did you do this?

Yeah, I wore a lot of hats for the Vikings. Starting in December of 1970 I was hired by the Vikings as a college scout. And after about five years, I was given the title Director of Player Personnel, which I kept up until probably about nine years ago and then for five years I was Vice President of Player Personnel.

How many Super Bowls were you a part of?

I was a part of three Super Bowls.

Were there any players who were a disappointment? Players who you thought would have been better than they turned out?

There were numerous ones. I would hate to name names. I think everybody has some players who don't pan out the way they thought they would, but for the most part, I was very fortunate to work with Jerry Reichow and we were able to draft and sign a lot of players who played a very long time in the National Football League.

Could you share with us some of the brighter spots who weren't drafted in the first round who turned out to be a plus for the team?

Well, you were probably as good an example as any, Matt. We got you in the second round and we thought that was a steal and we all know why that was. We had Sammy White in the second round—he was a great player for us. We got Jeff Wright who played defensive back for us as a free agent and he played a long, long time for us.

Were there any players who were not drafted who made the team and gave a contribution to the Vikings?

I think Jeff Wright is as good as anybody. A non-drafted guy that I was part of. Recently we were able to get guys like Spencer Johnson who is on our team right now and a couple of guys like Kelly, the wide receiver from Georgia Tech, he's been a good find for us. Of course we drafted Matt Birk as almost a free-agent but was a seventh-round draft choice. He's been an All-Pro center for us for quite a while. But you know, in thirty-four years that I have been around, there's a lot of guys I could name. We're fortunate enough that they work out, but you know lately, because you only have seven rounds, you are going to have more free agents that are going to make the team than twenty years ago when more were drafted in rounds.

What was, in the past, the highest draft round?

When I first came, I think it was like, seventeen and then we went down to twelve and now it's at seven.

What is the path to making the team? What does a prospective hopeful need to have to be a good professional player? What do you look for?

First of all, you have to have talent—that's the first thing you have to have. And I think you have to have talent in your athletic ability. You have to have adaptability, you have to adapt to the new way of doing things in the pros from college. You have to adapt to the number of games, you have to adapt to the strength and speed of players who you are playing against in the National Football League, because you are playing against the best football players in the world.

There's the discipline. When the players are hitting, you've got to discipline yourself to learn what you are supposed to do, spend the time to learn what you're supposed to learn. Be disciplined enough to do the things that they ask you to do, and then you have to have the ability. I think you've heard the term, "you can't make the club in the tub." You know, to make a good player, you have to be on the field to learn about the game better. So those are three things I think a guy has to have—athletic ability, adaptability, and durability.

In the draft that comes up each year, what preparations are involved in picking a player in the draft?

The process starts for us in the spring before the next draft. We have a meeting in May and we meet at the Combine we call Blesto, and those Combine scouts report to us, the upcoming prospects who they think might have the ability to play in the league. These guys have areas throughout the country and we kind of make out a schedule to see these guys. We start that in August, and the purpose of this is to decide whether these guys are as good or not as good as they have been reported to us that they are. Those people that do who are scouts like myself, called "Club Scouts." We'll also go to

Bowl games after the season's over and we'll evaluate players there, we'll evaluate them at the Combine, then we'll evaluate them again when we have their own school personal workout and then we'll meet for about two to three weeks before we get them all lined up in the positions. So it's just about a twelve-month process.

If there's anything you wanted to say to a young player who is going to come to the NFL, what would you share with him?
Prepare yourself to compete with the best football players in the world and do not, I don't care how high you're drafted, do NOT underestimate the people who you're going to be playing against.

KIRSTEN LINDBERG
BOBBE DAGGETT

ASSISTANT TO HEAD COACHE
FINANCIAL

Bobbe Daggett (left); Kirsten Lindberg (right),
photo taken 2005

Interview taped at Winter Park, Eden Prairie, Minnesota,
March 2005

How many years have you been employed by the Vikings, Kirsten?

At the end of April, it was twenty-six years.

How many years have you been employed by the Vikings, Bobbe?

At the end June, it was twenty-four years.

Are you guys true fans? Do you actually go to the games?

Kirsten: It's been many years since I've been to the games. I'm still a true fan, but I don't go to the games. I like staying home, in my jammies, closing the door and pulling the shades, and screaming all by myself. If I go to the game, I end up talking to people and I don't get to see the game.

Bobbe: I'm a true fan and I go to every game. Some of the pre-season games, I might not. It's very important to me who I go to the game with because I don't want to go to the game with a talker, I want somebody who's a fan, I want somebody who's positive who won't say anything negative about the Vikings.

What was your first position when you started with the Vikings?

Bobbe: I started in the finance department working for Harley Peterson, and I have had three bosses: Harley, my first one, Nick Valentine, and now Steve Poppin. And I've always worked in the finance department.

Kirsten: I actually started part-time before my twenty-six years. I worked on the switchboard at our old office on France Avenue on game day weekend. Then I started fulltime in April of 1979 in the ticket office with Terry Randolph and Jerry Christensen. I worked there until we got the new stadium and helped assign all the seats to the new stadium. I worked out there briefly, but I didn't want to work downtown. That's when they found a niche for me out at Winter Park at Public Relations for a couple years. I then went to work with Patty and Frank Gilliam and Jerry Reichow in personnel. I kind of helped out with the coaching department when Cathy MacMullan was here. And once Jerry Burns got the job, I started helping with the coaches.

Did you have to do anything with the scouting reports they sent out?

Kirsten: Well, it kind of evolved over the years. At one point I did all of the typing for all of the offense and defense and special teams. And we did the playbooks in house. And now I hardly do anything for the assistants. I work for strictly for Coach Tice and do all his scheduling and stuff. But I did, when Bob Schnelker was the offensive coordinator, work late on Monday, Tuesday, and Wednesday nights typing up the call sheets—on a typewriter, not a computer—so if there was a mistake the whole thing had to be typed again. Then I would run all of the scouting reports and stuff in the morning, but they did a lot of it by hand and by computer when Mike Harris was here. And then I went into special teams with Tom Batta, before I started working for Mike.

The guys in the locker room get their paychecks every week or every two weeks, so how many checks have been written over the years?

Bobbe: Oh, my gosh. I couldn't even guess. During the training camp, they get paid every week. And then once the season starts, they get a check every other week. And that goes from September to the last game of the season. And then there would be playoff checks, hopefully. So that times twenty-some years—that's quite a few checks.

What was the largest check written for a player?

Bobbe: Actually, I have not done payroll for the last five years. All I can remember is, the system that we had at the time when I was working, would not go over $999,999.99 So if a player had a check that was over that amount, then I had to cut two checks and that happened a lot.

Any favorite coaches that you guys like to work with, or looked up to?

Kirsten: Gosh, there are a lot. There have been a ton of coaches who have come through these doors and I still keep in touch with a lot of them. I always admired Bud [Grant] a lot . . . I was always afraid of him. When I first started, I barely made eye-contact. I'd put my head down, and now you just realize they're human with their foibles too. I think maybe Burnsie still may be the funniest man I've ever met in my life. And they remember me at Christmas every year, I talk to them a number of times. Tom Moore was the coordinator at Indianapolis, who still calls once a week and we chat. It's kind of fun. When I first started, the staff stayed here, nobody moved around. But now, we know people on all different staffs. I talked to Michael Archie about a week ago. I worked for Dennis [Green] for ten years who was great to us and I love working for Mike [Tice]. And Tony Dungy asked me to go to Tampa with him when he went. Lilliham, Pete Carroll, we've had great people. Really good, fun personalities.

Bobbe: I have to agree with Kirsten. We met a lot of really wonderful coaches. To single out one would be really hard to do. I like and respect Bud [Grant], but I like Jerry Burns because he was just the funniest guy. And our current coach, it's hard to beat him for personality. So it would be hard to pick one.

Did you know Max Winter, the original owner? What can you tell us about him?

Kirsten: He was a darling man. I adored Max. You know, the thing about him was he was a real people person. And some people are better with that stuff than others. He'd go to Hawaii every year in the winter, and when he returned, he would come through the office and shake everyone's hand and say "Hi" the morning that he came back. I admired him a lot, I liked him a lot.

Bobbe: He was a great guy. He always had stories to tell, just really good stories. He had a real thumbs-on here in the finance department because every check that I ever issued, he would personally sign. So I would write out checks weekly and take them down to his office and he would sit there and he would talk to me while he signed every one of these checks. And he pretty much knew everything that went on here, so it wasn't like current day owners where they manage from afar. He was really right on top of things.

Would you say that he was part of the community and was there a charity that he was known for?

I can't recall. We did the Children's Funds, an Evening with the Vikings, and I think those went to the Children's Funds and hospitals and stuff.

Working here with long hours, are you missed by your family, and are there any conflicts?

Kirsten: The only conflicts centered around family vacations when we had to plan around the draft or mini camp or stuff like that. I mean, I'm lucky being single. When I really worked the long hours, with the assistant coaches, I didn't have kids or a husband at home waiting for dinner and so it worked out really well. I know there were a lot of other people around the league who had to deal with that. And I never went to training camp either and now I do, with Mike. So, that would be difficult if I had a family.

Bobbe: Well, it's just my husband and me, and I work some late evenings and a few weekends during the latter part of the season. But I don't think he misses me. He can cook for himself.

Any good or bad memories of training camp?

Kirsten: I didn't think I would ever admit this, but it's kind of good to go to training camp. I never went before. We had runners going every day to make it work out for me, but Mike thought it was important that I be there. So I said, "Okay, but I better be busy because I don't want to sit and twiddle my thumbs," and that has never been a problem. It is busy, nonstop and there is just kind of a special camaraderie or togetherness. I mean, just everybody from players to coaches, to staff in the office. You kind of feel like you're working toward something. It's a good feeling.

Bobbe: I don't have to attend training camp at all, but every year, they would always take the office staff. Maybe we would go down there for a day, hop in a van or drive cars together, and there are some wonderful memories from that. As far as my connection with the training camp, the only difference between that time and the regular season is getting invoices approved and that would always be a kind of, I hate to use this term, but a black hole down in Mankato. If I send things down there, I might never see them again.

From seeing all the athletes who have come through here, what advice would you have for young hopefuls with aspirations of becoming a football player?

Kirsten: It always amazes me the opportunity that these players have and how few athletes get to this level, and I think even more so, years ago, players had more connection in the communities. Working with different charities and a lot of these guys don't avail themselves of that. I guess I would say get your degree and make commitments to the community. It will serve you well, because football doesn't last forever.

Bobbe: That's a very good point. I would also like to say that education is very important and to think about what you're going to do after football. Like Kirsten said, football doesn't last forever. And so many times players leave football and they don't know what they want to do. They struggle and they really have a hard time with that. I think all the time when they're playing, they should be thinking about what they're going to do afterward and not take for granted that they are professional athletes. Even though they make a lot of money when they're playing, they spend an awful lot. So the word of the day is "budget."

Is there anything you want to say that hasn't been said?

Kirsten: I would like to say, and I know Bobbe feels this way too, I'm glad I was here in the old days to experience that. It was such a small group of people and it was such a family kind of feeling with the owners we had. Now it's a business, it's a corporation. It's not bad, it's just different. So I'm glad that when I started I knew every single player, I knew their number, I knew what college they went to, and now there is so much change and transition, it's hard to get to know them. So I'm glad I got that experience.

Bobbe: I agree. It was kind of a small company. Everybody knew everybody and people helped each other out there. If I wasn't busy during the summer months, I was always asking if anyone needed help and so did Kirsten. You know, you just went from department to department to find things to do. Now it's so specialized and you're so concerned about your job. It's all about what you're going to do, and maybe not so much what everyone else does.

DENNIS RYAN

EQUIPMENT MANAGER

Photo taken 2005

S T A T S

HIGH SCHOOL
Name of School: Highland Park High
    School
Location of School: St. Paul, Minnesota
Graduation Year: 1977
Other sports played: Wrestling

COLLEGE
Name of School: University of Minnesota
    and St. Thomas College
Location of School: St. Paul, Minnesota
How long attended: 2 years at U of M,
    2 years at St. Thomas
Did you graduate? No

PRO
Position prior to Equipment Manager:
    Assistant Equipment Manager
Years as Head Equipment Manager: Since
    1981. 2005 will be 25th year.
How many head coaches? Bud Grant, Les
    Steckel, Bud Grant, Jerry Burns,
    Dennis Green and Mike Tice
All-time Best Draft Pick of Vikings: Fran
    Tarkenton
Best Draft Round of Lower Rounds: Milt
    Sunde
Best Free Agent: John Randle

What's your weekly schedule like to prepare for a game?

Our week starts Sunday night after a game, whether it's home or away. We come back and unload the truck, do the laundry, depending on where we play. It's more difficult with an outdoor grass game, obviously. And if it's at home, there are nearly two thousand towels to wash and fold. And that extends, obviously into Monday. We then get to Tuesday, which is our day off, and we do about a ten-hour day on our day off and the rest of the week are pretty much fourteen-hour days throughout the week. And each day we pack a few more items getting ready, preparing for the game; until Saturday they're moving into the Metrodome or taking our truck to the airport.

During that week, do you help out with the team on the field, and what are your responsibilities to the team while the team is practicing?

On the field, Aaron Neuman and I are out there observing practice. Participating in some of the drills to help coordinate, I guess, efficiency in the drills and then we're just out there making sure if any helmets break, pads break, or whatever else needs repair, we're going to repair it and then move all the dummies and sleds off the field once the team is done using them.

How did you learn this process? Give a little background on becoming the head equipment manager for the Vikings?

It's all, you know, job experience. It wasn't learned in school. It's just a matter of working with Stubby Eason for years at Midway Stadium, Met Stadium, and then moving out to here and just picking it up. And then, you know, as time has gone by, the job has definitely changed in different areas and certain responsibilities and whatnot, have evolved, certainly since the beginning.

How many years have you been with the organization?

I've been with the organization since 1975, part time and full time since 1979. I'll have been with the club . . . this will be my thirtieth year, I guess.

Which players didn't pick up their stuff around their lockers—who are the slobs?

There's a few of them. [Laughter.] A few would deny it and a few would be pretty proud of it. Jim Huff comes to mind as one of the guys who would be very proud. In fact, he got angry whenever we would dig his practice pants out of his locker and wash them. He never wanted his clothes washed and some of the other guys would complain.

Any particular stories that you want to share on equipment breaks or if somebody had a problem with their helmet or pads?

I guess that was pretty funny, not funny necessarily at the time, but we turned around one time and there were flames coming out of Doug Martin's helmet on the field in Cleveland—that had to be back around 1986-87—when Burnsie was head coach. It was a cold day, below zero, windchill near zero temperatures, and Doug Martin wanted to keep his helmet warm, so he set it up on top of the big burner on the sidelines with the flame coming out of it. It kept it warm, and it burned it up and of course Doug had the biggest head on the team, so we had to put the thing back together and refit it and everything else. It was quite a chore.

What size was his helmet?

Doug, he wore about a size 8 1/2. Not nearly as big as what we have Brian McKinnie wearing now, but at the time, Doug Martin was the first guy we had who had an extra large shell and was the only guy in that big of a shell for several years.

Have there ever been times when you packed the wrong type of shoes for the weather?

I guess the only thing that comes to mind with the shoes is, I was working for Stubby, it was 1987, we were playing San Diego out at the old Met, it started to rain, it started to sleet a little, and it was freezing up and Stubby was concerned we were going to need broomball shoes. The field was going to be icy, so he sent me back to Midway Stadium in his LTD car to go pick up the broomball shoes and hopefully get back there before the game started. As I was leaving the parking lot, it was sheer ice and Sid Hartman was on his way and in his usual fashion, was paying no attention to anybody, including the parking lot attendant. I couldn't move. I was on sheer ice. He saw me, slammed his brakes on, and barreled into me head on. He got out of his car and was quite upset, and told me it was my fault because nobody should leave the stadium at that time of day and the fans nearby who were starting their tailgate party, got on Sid. They got on him a little sports rendition, and Sid said, "I'll see you after the game in the locker room." Which by then all the players knew about it and he came in and starting giving me just all sorts of trouble. The players were all over him, in turn, and he had to leave.

What are some practical jokes you saw among the players in the locker room?

One thing that stands out is, in the old days, the guys would roll up their socks after practice and just rifle them at each other across the locker room. You know, soaking them in water, soaking them in pop and whatever else and wing them across. You think of a bunch of grown men having a sock fight almost daily after practice, well . . . you know.

It's also important to do a jersey count after practice. I know a bunch of guys probably put their jerseys in their bag and take them home and use them or whatever. It's something that's become a big issue with our equipment budget. We get a number of things provided through NFL contracts and what we do now more than anything is our marketing department will auction some items off and our community relations department will auction things off and the guys, we don't have trouble with them.

Probably the most elaborate practical joke ever pulled was on Burnsie. Back in training camp—and every training camp once he became the head coach—first thing in Mankato I'd have to do is drive down to Sears & Roebuck in Mankato and pick up a mannequin. Burnsie wanted that mannequin outfitted to look like Monte Kiffin. We'd put Monte Kiffin's shirt and pants on and we'd put a toupee on his head. You know, Burnsie wanted to have everybody think that Keith Millard and Monte got into a fight in the locker room. He then had Millard and Kiffin have a fight in the training room and it moved out into the hallway. Pretty soon they disappeared and everybody went to the practice field and pretty soon you heard a commotion up from the roof of Gage hall about fifteen stories up. The two of them were at the edge of the wall and Keith was just screaming at Monte and choking him or whatever and they disappeared back behind the chimney. A few minutes later, they re-emerged and this dummy came flying off the roof and Burnsie just got a hoot out of that and thought it was just the greatest thing. Everybody thought Millard had just tossed Monte off Gage Hall.

When the rookies come in, do they fit in right away? Does it take them a long time to understand the ropes and how it works here?

Most the guys are pretty quiet when they come in. A few guys stick out. Jessie Solomon was never quiet. Those guys are few and far between. Most guys come in and, no matter what their background is, they're quiet. They want to learn the ropes, they want to do what the veterans expect and generally, if they come in with kind of an attitude, they generally don't seem to stick around. There are very few of those guys, however.

The timing of you getting all the information and all the equipment you need for playing—are they usually waiting for you or are you usually waiting for the team or players to board the plane?

When we leave Minneapolis, we're already on the airplane before the players board. But on the road, generally the team is on the airplane waiting for us. They make sure they're well taken care of with fluids, hamburgers, pizza, and whatever else. They feed them pretty good so they're at least a little bit distracted while the plane is being loaded.

What time of day during the season do you come in?

During the season, between 5 and 5:30 AM.

And the time that you leave?

Generally, about 7:30-8:00 at night.

And during the off-season?

It's pretty much a normal work schedule. A nine-to-five, well, about 7-4 is what we generally work in the off-season.

Do you have any activities that you have that you like to do?

I've got three kids and those have been the activities. And they're all involved in athletics of one form or another and all three of them play hockey so we keep busy from October until springtime with hockey and then we've got baseball, softball, all sorts of other things. We've got a lot going on.

Did you have another job before this?

I really only had two jobs in my life prior to this. One was pumping gas at a gas station for about two weeks. The gas station went bankrupt and I had to get another job the next summer. I started working at a small stadium in St. Paul—Midway Stadium. I was on the ground crew and that's when Stubbie, the equipment manager, said he needed some help moving the training camp so it became where I worked two different jobs—on the grounds and during the football season, then would work part-time helping Stubbie in the locker room. That's how it all started. I can say I'm blessed that I found a great job at a young age and have been able to continue in that for my entire life.

Is there a message that you'd like to offer the kids who may aspire to do this job?

Hopefully when they watch these guys, they realize how much work these guys have put in. I've seen thousands of guys pass through this locker room and the few made it for an extended period of time who were able to make a great living at it, so be sure to get their education and have fun and play sports secondarily.

Any other interesting stories you want to share?

Burnsie's first game as a head coach, I was running down to the field, and as usual I'm the last one out of the locker room. I'm running down the tunnel at the Metrodome and there was Burnsie standing off to the corner with the security guard. I didn't think anything of it and continued running and I heard a, "Hey, boy! Hey, boy!" I turn around and he says, "Tell this 'blankity-blank' who the 'blankity-blank' I am."

"What do you mean?" I said.

"He won't let me on the field! Tell him who the heck I am!"

"That's our head coach Jerry Burns."

I had seen that security guard over the years but he'd never seen Burnsie because Burnsie was always up in the Press Box so he just thought that he was just some guy dressed up like a coach to sneak on to the field.

So did Jerry Burns ever get your name straight?

Everybody was a boy to him. When Fran Tarkenton was around, he always said things like "Hey, boy, you're not supposed to be in that area!"

SID HARTMAN

SPORTS WRITER
MINNEAPOLIS STAR TRIBUNE

Photo taken 2005

Interview taped at Winter Park, Eden Prairie, Minnesota, April 2005

How did you first get into sports reporting?

I hung around the newspaper from the time I was ten years old, selling papers and doing things like that. When I wasn't selling papers, I'd go upstairs to different sports departments. Finally in the early '40s they had an opening in the sports department and Dick Cullim hired me. I never graduated from high school, I got a good job as a newspaper guy, selling newspapers, delivering newspapers in cars to different stores and I also never went to college. This is my sixtieth year working in the Kohl's organization.

Your first time reporting for the Vikings was in 1961?

I've been reporting the Vikings ever since they got here.

Have you always had your column like it is today in the *Star Tribune*?

Yeah, since the late '40s, I've had that column.

In your column you cover everything in general, but you always have a comment about players who have retired or moved on in the sport. When did you start that part of it?

I try and keep in contact with all different guys. I go over to the University every day and I get to know these kids well and they'll keep in contact with me and let me know when they get a new job or if they retire from pro football or basketball or something like that, so I get a lot of emails and calls from these guys. They keep in contact.

Would you say you've stayed friends with all the people you've interviewed over the years?

You know my relationship in that locker room. All those guys trusted me explicitly. If you were out the night before with some woman, I didn't print that. If I was going to write something, I would check with the guys, I'd try to be fair and it wasn't always positive, but you knew it was accurate. That was the most important thing.

Is it a credit to your name and your reputation to be a man of your word?

First of all, I was the first guy to ever use a tape recorder. And when you get stuff taped, there is nothing out of context. When guys take stuff down and write stuff down, you get stuff out of context and when they get back to the office, they're not sure what that note was and they might screw it up. Well, I don't screw it up because I'd tape everybody and it'd be accurate and either I'd go back to the office and I'd transcribe it or I'd get somebody to transcribe it. So it was always accurate.

Was there a particular player in the locker room who gave you problems or didn't want you in the locker room?
Nobody, I don't think.

How did your center become the Sid Hartman Center?
Mike Tice did that. I knew Mike Tice as a player and that was his idea. It was strictly his idea and McCombs went for it.

At one time, you were probably the only reporter who could walk through the locker room, and go upstairs and see Bud Grant. Is that right?
Yeah, well, Bud and I go back a long time and we're very close friends. I was honored to be Bud's presenter in the Hall of Fame and I think this thing exists because of all the coaches. Not with Denny Green for the first six months that he was here but now he found out that he could trust me and stuff like that. It's never been any different here.

Let's talk about Bud's induction into the Hall of Fame. How special was that for him to ask you to introduce him?
I never believed it was going to happen. When I called him up, I said, "Who's going to introduce you?"

"You," he said.

"You're out of your mind. You're kidding me." I know his wife almost as well as I know him, we went out together a lot when they were courting each other, so she said, "yeah, he always said you'd be the guy." I was very honored. I'm the first sports writer to ever do that.

How do you have time for your family when you have to report, when you're on call, or at the games?
I find a lot of time for my family. I've got five great grandkids and a daughter and a son. I spend as much time with them as anyone else does. You can do both if you allocate your time and know what you're doing, there is no problem at all. I mean, I don't find that a problem.

Is there someone special that comes to your mind as the greatest interview you've had?

The craziest interview I ever had was with Joe Namath. The Giants were playing the Jets in New York and I went out there to cover it because it was Tarkenton's first game, and I got to know Joe Namath real well through Cleve Rush who was his coach, who I just got to know along the line. He coached at Toledo and at Ohio State, so Namath turned out to be a good friend of mine. I was walking by the shower and he said, "Hey, Sid, come here. I'm not talking to anybody, but I'll talk to you. Put your tape recorder in here if you want to talk to me." So I got half wet in the shower and I got the interview.

How do you remember all these guys over the years?

I had a third grade teacher, named Mrs. Nettleton, and one of my buddies found a broken watch on the playground at Harrison Grade School, and he put the watch on even though it didn't work. But Mrs. Nettleton thought the watch worked because this kid was always looking at it. One day she said, "Bill, I hope when you get a job, you aren't looking at your watch all the time." Well I got that job. Getting to know guys like you, I've known you as a good friend for a long time, I can call you anytime, and I have that same relationship with most of the people.

Is there anything that you want to share with the readers about the Vikings that they might not know?

Well, the Super Bowl losses. I think Alan Page had the greatest quote for some guy that came to him and said "How about you lose another Super Bowl?"

"I tell you what," he said, "why don't you go to training camp and ask every player on every team, 'You can go to the Super Bowl, but you're going to lose.' Do you think they'll say yes?" Just getting to the Super Bowl is great. I consider all the players—I'm not trying to sound egotistical—good friends who didn't question me or hold back what they said to me. And that to me is a big, big thing.

So that friendship with the Vikings is what means the most to you over the years?

The Vikings mean something special because I played a part in helping to get them here. Max Winter and I probably did more work than any one guy in getting them here. In fact, George Halas, the American Football League was suing the National Football League when the Vikings came in here, and George got up in court as he was being questioned and said, "Do you know a guy named Sid Hartman in Minneapolis?"

"Well, who's that guy?" they said.

"If you had him chase you like he chased me you would probably give up and help him get a franchise."

And that's what I did.

Other Books from Crotalus Publishing

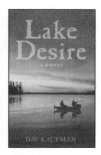

Lake Desire by Dāv Kaufman
Drama/Fiction, 240 pages, hardcover, 5.5" x 8.5", ISBN 0-9741860-0-7

This touching novel chronicles the interconnected stories of twelve residents of the small fishing town of Desire, Minnesota, after a boating accident takes the life of Elle Ravenwood, the town's most beloved resident. Bear, a biker and tattoo artist, has made it his religion to sit on a dock on the shores of Lake Desire every morning to write of the melancholy magic that swept over the town after Elle's death, and gives all of them the power to change their lives.

The Long Ride Home: A Life in the Minnesota Music Scene by Mick Sterling
Regional/Music, 240 pages, paperback, 5.5" x 8.5", ISBN 0-9741860-5-8

This is the intriguing story of a Minneapolis soul singer doing his best to thrive in clubland. Penned by one of the most recognizable voices in the Twin Cities music scene, Mick Sterling, this book is filled with moments of insight, surprising tenderness, dry humor, and confessions from a singer who's played thousands of gigs in everything from smoky bars to huge outdoor festivals. You'll never watch a band onstage in quite the same way again.

Roadsides: Images of the American Landscape by Kelly Povo
Photojournal/Nonfiction, 112 pages, hardcover, 10" x 8", ISBN 0-9741860-3-1

Through images of diners and cafes, bowling alleys and bars, drive-ins and motels, photographer Kelly Povo has spent the past twenty years capturing the essence of these places on the road. Her photographs invite us to revel in their unique designs, and perhaps even find memories in these "slices of Americana" that dot the American landscape. Featuring informative, historical, and enlightening text by Bruce Johansen.

North: Stories and Photographs by Dāv Kaufman, Martin Springborg, Kelly Povo, Phyllis Root, Dr. Daniel Keyeler, Dr. Barney Oldfield, Terry Pepper, Bill Marchel, Jeff Richter
Nonfiction, 112 pages, hardcover, 11" x 8.5", ISBN 0-9741860-4-X

Through a selection of talented writers and photographers, the North is embodied in stories and photographs of the pursuit of albino deer in the central woods of Wisconsin, of the lifelong search to encounter a moose in the wilds of nothern Minnesota, of trailing timber rattlesnake in the Mississippi River bluffs in south-eastern Minnesota, and in many others. Each of the artist's chapters offers a dramatic perspective of the region we love—each of them welcoming us North.

Order direct from www.crotaluspublishing.com
or wherever books are sold.

AUTOGRAPHS